Fig. 1.

Fig. 2.

Fig. 5.

Fig. 4.

Fig. 3.

Fig. 7.

Fig. 6.

How To Know

THE

LICHENS

How To Know

THE
LICHENS

Mason E. Hale

Smithsonian Institute

WM. C. BROWN COMPANY PUBLISHERS
Dubuque, Iowa

ISBN 0–697–04822–5 (Paper)
ISBN 0–697–04823–3 (Cloth)

Library of Congress Catalog Card Number 72-89535

THE PICTURED-KEY NATURE SERIES

How To Know The—

AQUATIC PLANTS, Prescott, 1969
BEETLES, Jaques, 1951
BUTTERFLIES, Ehrlich, 1961
CACTI, Dawson, 1963
EASTERN LAND SNAILS, Burch, 1962
ECONOMIC PLANTS, Jaques, 1948, 1958
FALL FLOWERS, Cuthbert, 1948
FRESHWATER ALGAE, Prescott, 1954, 1970
FRESHWATER FISHES, Eddy, 1957, 1969
GRASSES, Pohl, 1953, 1968
GRASSHOPPERS, Helfer, 1963, 1972
IMMATURE INSECTS, Chu, 1949
INSECTS, Jaques, 1947
LAND BIRDS, Jaques, 1947
LICHENS, Hale, 1969
LIVING THINGS, Jaques, 1946
MAMMALS, Booth, 1949, 1970
MARINE ISOPOD CRUSTACEANS, Schultz, 1969
MOSSES AND LIVERWORTS, Conard, 1944, 1956
NON-GILLED FLESHY FUNGI, Smith-Smith, 1973
PLANT FAMILIES, Jaques, 1948
POLLEN AND SPORES, Kapp, 1969
PROTOZOA, Jahn, 1949
ROCKS AND MINERALS, Helfer, 1970
SEAWEEDS, Dawson, 1956
SPIDERS, Kaston, 1953, 1972
SPRING FLOWERS, Cuthbert, 1943, 1949
TAPEWORMS, Schmidt, 1970
TREMATODES, Schell, 1970
TREES, Miller-Jaques, 1946, 1972
WATER BIRDS, Jaques-Ollivier, 1960
WEEDS, Wilkinson-Jaques, 1959, 1972
WESTERN, TREES, Baerg, 1955, 1973

10/76

INTRODUCTION

Lichens are known to most naturalists as unusual but somewhat mysterious plants. Part of the mystery lies in the fact that there are but few reliable books about lichens written for beginning students. Many people collect lichens but are soon frustrated when they try to put names on them. Books for identification are so badly out of date, overly technical, or inaccurate that one has little chance of correctly naming an unknown specimen.

Fortunately, detailed studies of several large groups of lichens have been published in the last ten years. With these studies as a base, we have been able to construct keys to most of the foliose and fruticose lichens of North America, which are, it is hoped, as useful as those available for fungi, mosses, algae, and higher plants. These keys should enable a student to identify the North American lichens from the boreal forests of Canada southward to Florida and Baja California. Crustose forms are not included because they are far too numerous to combine with the macrolichens and often too little known in North America to present in workable keys. Though imperfect, Fink's *Lichen Flora of North America* is still the best reference for keying out crustose genera and species.

There are of course certain inherently difficult genera of macrolichens for which no recent taxonomic treatments are available, in particular, *Collema*, *Ramalina*, and *Usnea*. These groups are summarized rather broadly and we make no claim for completeness here.

Illustrations have been a constant problem in preparing this book. Lichens are not easy to draw, and indeed very few satisfactory drawings have ever been published compared with other plant groups. Most lichenologists have merely written descriptions without illustrations or at best with halftone photographs. I have been fortunate, through grants from the Smithsonian Institution, to obtain the services of Miss Nancy Halliday, who drew many of the Cladonias, Mr. Ernani Menez, Mr. Jack Schroeder, whose habitat drawings of the foliose lichens are outstanding, and other artists as indicated. The remaining species have been illustrated with photographs.

The preliminary keys were tested by the lichen classes of 1963 and 1966 at the Itasca Biological Station, University of Minnesota, and the class of 1968 at the University of Michigan Biological Station. Miss Beth Denison assembled most of the data for the distribution maps and helped in unraveling several difficult genera. Dr.

Barbara Moore has been especially helpful in the final preparation of the keys. Dr. I. Mackenzie Lamb generously allowed me to use his unpublished data on *Stereocaulon* in North America. Dr. Howard Sierk read the section on *Leptogium* and Mr. Isao Yoshimura gave advice on the *Cladonia* keys. Drs. Sam Shushan and W. A. Weber both added unpublished data on the distribution of western lichens. Mrs. Eleanor Stubblefield and Mrs. Anita Brooks were of invaluable assistance in general editing and typing of the final manuscript.

Collecting lichens in Minnesota

CONTENTS

I Rhyme With 'Liken'

MOSS   LICHEN   FUNGUS

THE
LICHENS

WHAT ARE LICHENS

Everyone is familiar with plants as green chlorophyll-containing organisms that manufacture their own food. A lichen is also a plant, but a very special kind, for when we dissect and examine it under a microscope, we find that it is composed of two completely different organisms, microscopic green or blue-green **algae** that are related to free-living algae and colorless **fungal threads** called hyphae (Fig. 1). These two components grow together in a harmonious association referred to as symbiosis, or more simply a "living together." Lichen symbiosis, however, differs basically from all other kinds in that a new plant body, the **thallus**, is formed, and this thallus has no resemblance at all to either a fungus or

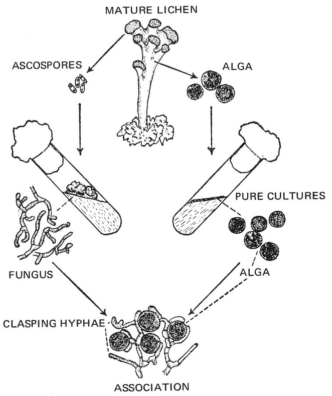

Figure 1. Steps in separating and reconstituting lichen components.

1

an alga growing alone. This new composite organism behaves as a single independent plant, the green alga manufacturing sugars by photosynthesis and the fungus living off these foodstuffs and making up the bulk of the plant body. The alga and fungus can be separated artificially and cultured in test tubes (Fig. 23) but most attempts to recombine them to form a new lichen have been unsuccessful.

Lichens are classified as **cryptogams**, a class of lower plants that includes algae, fungi, and mosses. Technically they are placed with the fungi, but in the minds of most laymen they are often lumped with the mosses. True mosses differ in having primitive leaves and stems and are dark green. Lichens lack differentiation into leaves and stems and have distinctive pale yellowish green or mineral gray colors. The non-lichenized fungi (Fig. 2), the cup fungi, mush-

Figure 2. A cup fungus (left) and a gill fungus.

rooms, bracket fungi, etc., lack a green layer of algae internally and tend to grow on dead trees and rotten logs or humus in dank woods. They are often soft and fleshy and, except for the hard bracket fungi, usually shrivel when dried. Lichens, by comparison, most often grow in open or exposed sunny places and appear unchanged with drying and aging.

WHAT TO LOOK FOR

Lichen thalli are generally round in outline, between 1 cm and 30 cm in diameter, and scattered, although clusters of thalli may fuse and cover large areas of tree trunks or rocks. The most easily recognized features of the thallus are growth form, color, and size, which taken together can be used to tell genera apart in the field. Identification to species can be done in many cases with the naked eye, but some important characters are too small to be seen without a magnifying lens. While a stereoscopic binocular scope of 10-30X is ideal for a serious student, such expensive equipment will not be found outside of college or high school laboratories. An ordinary hand lens of 2-10X, costing less than $5-$10, and a good desk lamp will suffice. The desired level of magnification is usually indicated in the keys. Never use more than 10X, even though most binocs go to 20X-30X, unless so instructed. A compound microscope with a magnification of 100-200X is required for anatomical and spore sections and for microchemical tests.

Colors of Lichens

The colors of lichens are distinctive yet rather subtle and hard to describe. It is extremely important to judge colors only after the thallus is air-dried. If wet or moist, the thallus may turn green. The reason is that the normally opaque upper cortex becomes translucent on wetting, bringing out the green of the chlorophyll-containing algae within the thallus.

The following colors are characteristic for lichens and are shown in the frontispiece: Mineral or greenish gray (1 and 2); greenish yellow, not at all grass green (unless wet) and technically described as lumiere yellow or sea-foam green (3); sulphur or lemon yellow (4); orange (5); brown (6), with variations from tan, straw, buff, chestnut or coffee brown to blackish brown; and slate bluish or lead colored (7) as in many gelatinous lichens. When color is used in the keys, the thallus being identified should be matched with the color chart in bright light.

Growth Forms

Growth form means the overall shape and configuration of the lichen thallus. There are three major types: **foliose** (leaf-like), **fruticose** (shrubby or hair-like), and **crustose** (crust-like). A fourth type, the **squamulose** lichens, may also be recognized.

Foliose Lichens

Foliose lichens are flattened and prostrate with an upper surface that is different from the lower, either in color or surface features (Fig. 3). The thallus expands outward from the center as it grows, becoming more or less round in outline. There are definite maximum diameters for these lichens and they can be grouped roughly in size classes as small (1-2 cm in diameter), medium-sized (3-12 cm), and large (13-30). The thallus is usually attached by rhizines over most or all of the lower surface. Rock tripes differ in having only a single central point of attachment below, the umbilicus (see Fig. 27).

Figure 3.   Top (left) and bottom surfaces of a foliose lichen (*Parmelia tinctorum*).

How closely a thallus is attached to a rock or to tree bark is an important character that calls for a certain amount of personal judgment. Appressed or closely adnate thalli can usually not be peeled from rock or bark without damage. Adnate, loosely adnate, or loosely attached thalli can be removed with a knife or by hand. While pieces of the substratum attached to the thallus may be valuable for reference in ecological studies, it is rather difficult to prepare specimens on bulky pieces of bark or rock for your collection.

The typical foliose thallus is divided into numerous branches called **lobes.** The lobes tend to elongate and fork again and again. Lobe width is a very important character. It should be measured carefully with a millimeter ruler as indicated in the keys, taking the average for several lobes. **Narrow lobes** (Fig. 4) are 0.1 to 2.0 mm wide and tend to be linear or strap-shaped with blunt or angled tips. **Broad lobes** (Fig. 4) range from 3 to 20 mm wide and are more irregular in width with rounded or rotund tips.

Margins of lobes are smooth or variously indented, varying from crenate to dentate, dissected, finely divided, or lacerate. Cilia are hair-like structures that occur in many species (see Fig. 404) and are from 0.5-6.0 mm long. They are very important in identifying lichen species.

The Upper Surface—The degree of wrinkling or ridging of the upper surface of lobes is important. The cortex surface, as seen

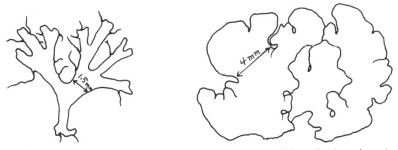

Figure 4. Narrow linear lobes (left) and broad rotund lobes, showing where to measure lobe width.

with a hand lens, may be continuous, without breaks or markings, or distinctly cracked (Fig. 5A), white-spotted or with irregular white markings (Fig. 5B). Actual tiny white pores through the cortex, barely visible to the naked eye, are called **pseudocyphellae** (Fig. 5C). The thin hoary white surface layer so typical of *Physcia* species is called **pruina** (Fig. 5D). An unusual feature of the upper cortex of *Peltigera* is **cephalodia** (see Fig. 402), tiny warty thalli 0.5-1.0 mm in diameter containing blue-green algae.

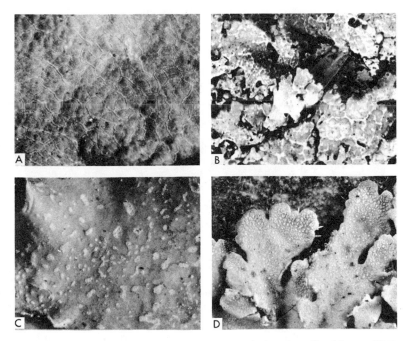

Figure 5. Surface features. A, reticulately cracked cortex; B, white markings and ridging; C, white pores (pseudocyphellae); D, pruina (all enlarged 2-5X).

The Lower Surface—The lower surface of lobes has a number of characters that are used in classifying lichen species. The color varies from jet black to some shade of brown, buff, ivory, or rarely white. The very edges of the lobes may be bare and paler than the central part, even turning white or mottled. Most of the Peltigeras have distinct veins (see Fig. 428). If the thallus lacks a lower cortex, the white cottony fibrous medulla is easily seen. If a cortex is present, the surface is smooth, shiny, and sparsely to densely covered with rhizines or tomentum.

Rhizines are compacted strands of fungal hyphae, produced from the lower cortex, which attach the thallus to the substratum. They may be simple (Fig. 6), once or twice furcate, or more elaborately branched, either dichotomously or squarrosely (see Fig. 93). Branching patterns are very important and must be determined with a hand lens. Rhizines are most commonly black, but if the lower cortex is pale, they too may be pale.

Tomentum (Fig. 6C, D) differs from rhizines in basic structure. Examined under a microscope, tomentum appears as thin chains of cells without any branching patterns. It forms a pale brown to black felty mat over the lower surface. There can be confusion with rhizines, which are much thicker and more compacted, but with practice these structures can be recognized with a hand lens.

A   B   C   D

Figure 6. Lower surface. A, B, rhizines; C, tomentum; D, tomentum with cyphellae (all enlarged 5-10X).

Distinct pores occur in the lower surface of several genera that have tomentum. Unique cyphellae (Fig. 6D), sunken pits scattered among the felty tomentum which can be easily seen without a hand lens, distinguish the genus *Sticta* from all other lichens. These pores differ from pseudocyphellae in being larger and in having a cortical layer. The genus *Pseudocyphellaria* always has tiny pseudocyphellae scattered over the lower surface as well as sometimes on the upper surface. Other foliose genera, especially *Parmelia,* may have them on the upper surface.

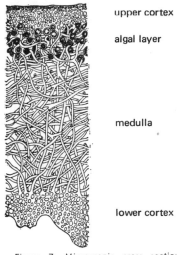

upper cortex

algal layer

medulla

lower cortex

Figure 7. Microscopic cross section of a typical foliose lichen.

Internal Structure of the Thallus—Internal structures must be examined with a compound microscope. Freehand sections can be made with a razor blade after some practice or a freezing microtome can be used. Ordinary histological staining procedures may be followed to prepare permanent slides. Safranin, fast green, orcein, and other stains work well. The interior of the thallus in **stratified** lichens consists of an upper **cortex** of compressed cells, a thin but distinct **algal layer** below this, a thick loosely packed **medulla** composed of hyphal strands, and a lower cortex which may be lacking in some groups (Fig. 7). The usual alga is a unicell, *Trebouxia.* Though usually white, the medulla on rare occasions is pigmented orange or yellow. **Unstratified** lichens have no differentiation into algal layer and medulla. The algae (*Nostoc, Stigonema,* and other blue-greens) are intermingled with the hyphae in a dark uniform layer (see Fig. 427). These are also called gelatinous because of the tendency of the thallus to expand and become somewhat jelly-like when wet. They are often dark brown or black.

Fruticose Lichens

Fruticose lichens consist of simple or divided branches that are round in cross section or somewhat flattened with only weak differences between the top and bottom. They are bushy, hairy, or strap-shaped, attached at the base to the substratum or growing free without any attachment. They may hang down or stand erect (Fig. 8). Growth occurs at the branch tips, and some of these lichens may grow to be 5-10 feet long. Rhizines are of course lacking and cilia are extremely rare. The interior of the branches is divided into a medulla in the center and a thin algal layer below the outer cortex. *Usnea,* however, is unusual in having a dense central cord (Fig. 9), whereas *Cladonia* has a hollow center.

Figure 8. Fruticose growth forms: *Usnea hirta* (left) and *Cladonia*.

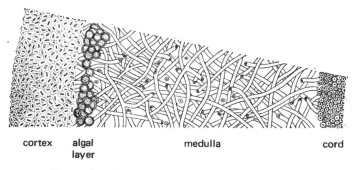

cortex   algal   medulla   cord
           layer

Figure 9. Microscopic radial cross section of an *Usnea*.

Squamulose Lichens

Squamules are small lobe-like structures that have an upper cortex, algal layer, and a medulla but lack a lower cortex and rhizines. They are characteristic of the primary thallus of *Cladonia* (Fig. 10), but also occur in some species of *Lecidea* and *Dermatocarpon*. In general squamules are 1-10 mm long and clumped into mats several centimeters across.

Crustose Lichens

Although true crustose lichens as a group are not included in this book, several species of *Lecanora, Rinodina, Placopsis,* and

Figure 10. Squamules of a *Cladonia* (X2).

Caloplaca, with more or less distinctly lobed margins are included in these keys. The central part of the thallus is crustose, often chinked (Fig. 11), fissured, or areolate, and very firmly attached to the substratum. Except for the lack of a lower cortex and rhizines, they come very close to the adnate or appressed foliose types. True crustose lichens may also have a rather thick thallus but the margins will always be unlobed and sometimes fade into the substratum or become indistinct (Fig. 11). It is impossible to remove them from the substratum without destroying the thallus. One crustose lichen deserves special mention. This is *Lepraria aeruginosa,*

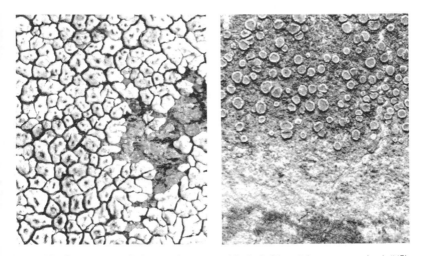

Figure 11. Crustose growth forms: *Acarospora hilaris* (left) and *Lecanora sambuci* (X5).

a fragile powdery whitish or greenish crust that is found very frequently on rocks, soil, or tree bases in shady places.

Isidia and Soredia

The two most important diagnostic characters for all lichen
groups are **isidia** and **soredia**, which are unique to lichens. They
must be recognized without hesitation and distinguished clearly.

Isidia are cylindrical outgrowths from the upper cortex, scattered
more or less evenly over the upper surface (Fig. 12). Since they

A   B
Figure 12. Isidia of *Pseudevernia consocians*. A, X1/2; B, X10.

are only up to 0.5 mm high, one should examine them with a hand
lens. They may be simple or branched, sparse to dense, papillate,
globular, tubercular, course, granular, even somewhat sorediate,
or dorsiventral or flattened (see Fig. 118). Isidia break away from
the thallus and leave a scar.

By contrast, soredia originate in the medulla and erupt at the
lobe surface as a powder, which is easily brushed off (Fig. 13).

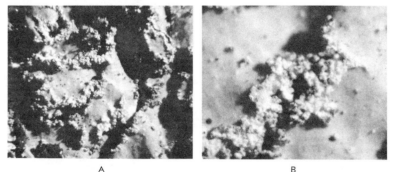

A   B
Figure 13. Soredia of *Parmelia fraudans*. A, X2; B, X10.

When this powder is examined under a microscope, we see aggregated clumps of a few algae closely surrounded by hyphae. Masses of soredia on the thallus surface are visible to the naked eye but should be examined with a hand lens in case of doubt. They often occur in definite forms, called **soralia,** which may be round or linear and occur on the lobe surface or tips (see Figs. 48A-D). Diffuse soredia not organized into soralia form over the whole thallus in many Cladonias.

Reproductive Structures

The most easily recognized reproductive structures are **apothecia** (Fig. 14A). These cup- or disc-shaped bodies, 1-20 mm in diameter,

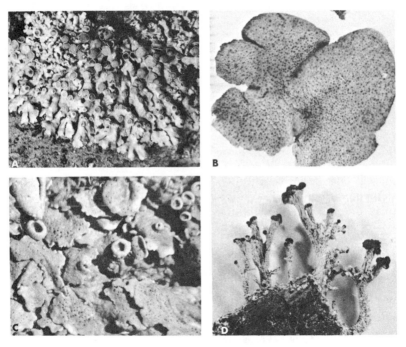

Figure 14. Fruiting bodies. A, apothecia of *Physcia stellaris;* B, perithecia of *Dermatocarpon miniatum;* C, pycnidia of *Parmelia bolliana;* D, apothecia on podetia of *Cladonia cariosa* (all X2).

usually occur on the upper surface, more rarely along lobe margins, as in *Cetraria,* on the lower surface, as in *Nephroma,* or at tips of branches (Fig. 14D). The apothecial disc is usually some shade of brown or blackish brown, rarely orange or yellowish or whitish.

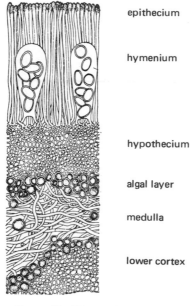

epithecium

hymenium

hypothecium

algal layer

medulla

lower cortex

Figure 15. Microscopic cross section of an apothecium.

The disc, when sectioned, shows a uniform layer of sterile threadlike **paraphyses** and scattered asci under the microscope. Each **ascus** contains 1-8, rarely more, **spores** (Fig. 15). The most important characters of spores are number of cross walls (septation) and color, which separate lichens into genera. In practice, however, when identifying foliose or fruticose lichen species, we do not use spores very often.

A second kind of reproductive structure is the **perithecium,** a flask-shaped structure buried within the thallus of *Dermatocarpon,* a foliose lichen, and of many custose genera. It appears at the upper surface as black dots (Fig. 14B). When sectioned, perithecia will be seen to contain typical paraphyses, asci, and spores. They may be confused with the much more widespread pycnidia (Fig. 14C), similarly immersed flask-shaped structures found in almost all genera. The pycnidia differ in containing numerous free, simple **microconidia,** only a few microns long and often very difficult to see in the microscope without good lighting (see Fig. 413).

The reproduction of lichens in nature is a mystery. Soredia, isidia, and thallus fragments can all act as vegetative propagules and when dislodged apparently resume growth to form a new thallus. Sexual reproduction in which spores form a new thallus and recombine with algae is theoretically possible, but no one has ever been able to prove that this happens in nature.

HOW TO MAKE CHEMICAL TESTS

Chemistry is not an important character in most plants groups, but in lichens it is a useful and practical means of identifying species.

Lichens produce unique chemical substances, most of them weak phenolic or fatty acids which are deposited on the surface of the hyphae. The main classes of substances are shown in Fig. 16. Each lichen usually has a constant chemical makeup so that the same species will give the same test, no matter where it was collected. This means that we can identify lichens more accurately by checking the chemical composition. Moreover, species that are easily confused without careful study, such as *Physcia aipolia* (medulla KOH+ yellow) and *P. stellaris* (medulla KOH−), are quickly separated by simply applying a drop of KOH to the medulla of unknown specimens. Some species, however, that are identical in appearance, have different chemistry. These "chemical species," which can be separated only by a chemical test, are mentioned in the keys where they occur.

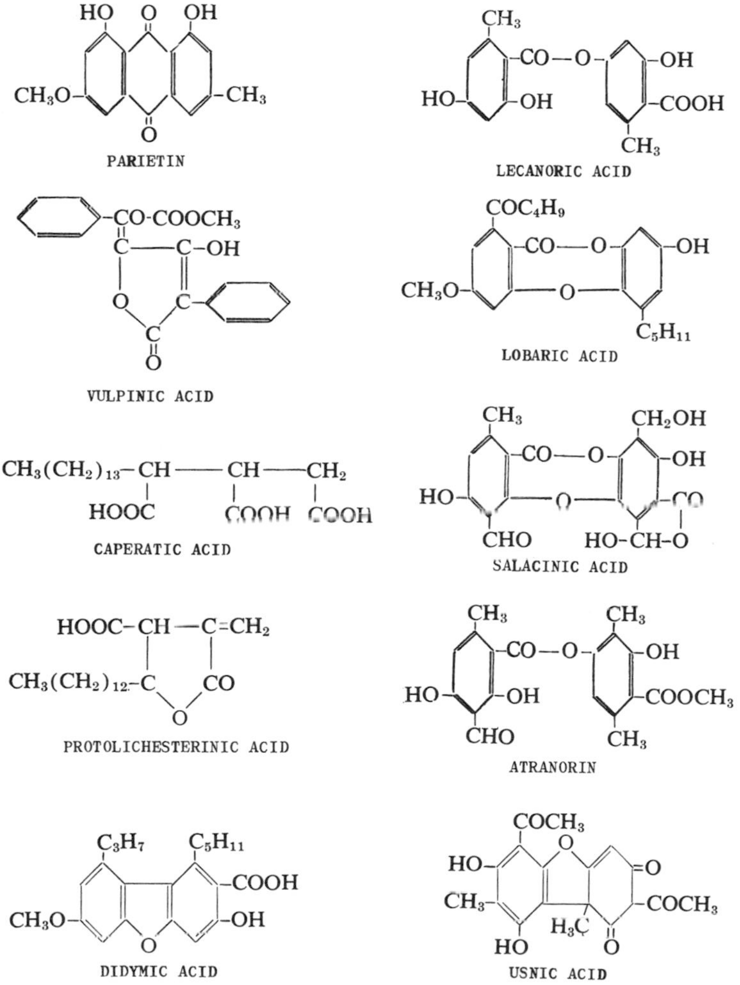

Figure 16. Structural formulae of some common lichen acids.

Color Tests

A color test is made simply by applying a drop of reagent on the thallus surface or exposed medulla. If the test is positive, there will be a rapid color change, usually red or yellow; if negative, nothing happens. Ideally the tests should be done under a low-power stereoscopic scope, leaving both hands free to apply the reagent, but a hand lens will be satisfactory with practice.

Three different reagents are used: calcium hypochlorite (bleaching powder, abbreviated C), potassium hydroxide (caustic lye, abbreviated K or KOH), and paraphenylenediamine (P). Calcium hypochlorite is a white pungent powder that should be mixed with water fresh each day. It deteriorates quickly and will give no reaction if spent. Various other powdered or liquid bleaches with a calcium or sodium hypochlorite base may be substituted and can be purchased in grocery stores.

Potassium hydroxide comes as dry sticks that should be stored in tightly closed bottles. Small pieces can be broken off and dissolved in water to make a fairly concentrated solution which is stable for several months. This chemical is caustic and should be handled carefully with tweezers or gloves. It can be bought in drugstores or chemical supply stores.

Paraphenylenediamine is a dark powder prepared for the tests by dissolving a pinch in 5-10 ml of ethyl alcohol (denatured alcohol or rubbing alcohol or even acetone, if nothing else is available). This reagent can only be purchased at a chemical or medical supply company. It must also be handled with great care because the spilled solution or powder will discolor and ruin clothing and paper. The powder should not be inhaled. Many students will have diffi-

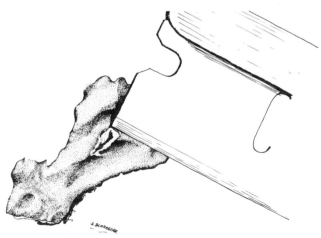

Figure 17. Scraping a cortex with a razor blade to prepare for a color test.

culty purchasing this reagent and the keys were designed to require as little use of it as possible.

Color tests are usually made in the medulla but also on the upper cortex. Under a lens, carefully scrape away part of the upper cortex with a razor blade to expose an area of white medulla about 2 square millimeters (Fig. 17). The reagents are applied with a very thin pipette or medicine dropper and any color change noted as the reagent is being applied. When K is added to the upper cortex, a spurious yellowish color will sometimes develop after a few seconds because the underlying green algae become moist. This false reaction must be carefully distinguished from the true immediate K+ yellow test caused by atranorin. Whenever there is doubt, a microchemical test would decide the issue by definitely showing the presence or absence of atranorin.

Microchemical Tests

It is entirely possible to identify lichens without ever making a microchemical test, and indeed most lichenologists use only the color tests. The keys in this book were constructed specifically to avoid involved tests. The value of microchemical tests, however, lies in their use to make positive identification of acids causing a particular color reaction. For example, since lecanoric and gyrophoric acid both react C+ red, only a microchemical test will distinguish them accurately. A serious student will not long be satisfied simply to make color tests. The notes below provide a brief introduction to microchemical methods. Unfortunately there is no complete summary on this subject. Most of the information has been published piecemeal in journals that are difficult to find. Brief summaries are presented in Hale's *Lichen Handbook* and in the *Biology of Lichens,* in Thomson's *Cladonia* book, and in Taylor's *Lichens of Ohio.*

Crystal Tests

In a crystal test, the acid is dissolved from small fragments of the thallus with acetone, and the crude residue that remains is recrystallized from various reagents on a microscope slide. The reagents in common use are abbreviated as follows and mixed in the volume ratios indicated:

> G.E. (glycerin-acetic acid, 3:1)
> G.A.W. (glycerin-95% alcohol-water, 1:1:1)
> G.A.o-T. (glycerin-alcohol-o-toluidine, 2:2:1)
> G.A.An. (glycerine-alcohol-aniline, 2:2:1)
> G.A.Q. (glycerine-alcohol-quinoline, 2:2:1)

These reagents are conveniently stored in brown dropper-bottles of 50 to 100 ml capacity and except for G.E. and G.A.W. should be prepared fresh every 3 to 6 months. o-Toluidine, aniline, and quinoline may be obtained from chemical supply houses. Acetone is sold in drugstores.

Fragments of the lichen thallus are heaped in the center of a microscope slide, and drops of acetone (or benzene for some acids) are added several times (Fig. 18). After the acetone evaporates, there should be a whitish or yellowish powdery (rarely gummy) ring of residue. (If no residue forms, do not attempt any tests.) The thallus fragments are carefully brushed away, a small drop of reagent put on a coverslip, and the coverslip placed over the residue. The slide is gently heated over an alcohol lamp, low Bunsen flame, or match until bubbles just begin to form. On cooling a few minutes, crystals will begin to form first around the undissolved residue, later at the perimeter of the coverslip. The shape and color of the crystals are determined under a low-power microscope (100X), and the crystals identified by comparison with photographs. A key to the more common acids is outlined below with their color reactions and crystal shapes, where appropriate. Those without a crystal test indicated should be examined with chromatography. It is best to practice first with lichens of known or proven composition.

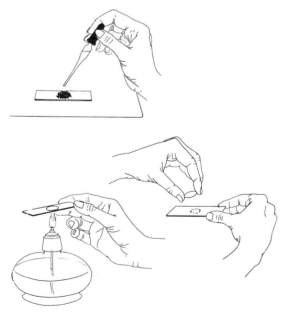

Figure 18. Steps in making a crystal test.

Pigments

Orange or red pigments, K+ purple: Parietin, rhodophyscin, solorinic acid.

Yellow pigments, K— (or yellowish): Calycin, pinastric acid, pulvic acid, usnic acid (straight yellow needles in G.E., Fig. 19A), vulpinic acid.

Colorless Substances

K+ yellow or yellow turning red: Atranorin (straight needles in G.E., yellow curved needle clusters in G.A.o-T., Fig. 19B), baeomycic acid, galbinic acid (deep yellow warts in G.A.o-T. scattered on atranorin crystals), norstictic acid (4-angled yellow lamellae in G.A.o-T., Fig. 19C), physodalic acid, salacinic acid (yellow orange boats in G.A.o-T., Fig. 19D), stictic acid (colorless hexagons in G.A.o-T., Fig. 19E), and thamnolic acid (yellow fascicles in G.A.o-T. with bubbling).

K— (or brownish), P+ yellow, orange, or red: fumarprotocetraric acid, pannarin, protocetraric acid (yellow warts in G.A.o-T., Fig. 19F), psoromic acid.

K—, P—, C+ pink or red: Anziaic acid, gyrophoric acid (warts in G.E., Fig. 19G), lecanoric acid (curved needle clusters in G.A.W. and G.E., Fig. 19H), olivetoric acid (gummy residue, long curved needles in G.A.W., Fig. 20A), scrobiculin.

K—, P—, C+ green: Didymic acid, strepsilin.

K—, P—, C—, KC+ pink or red: Alectoronic acid (gummy residue, small fan-shaped lamellae in G.A.W., Fig. 20B), cryptochlorophaeic acid (long curved needle clusters in G.A.W., Fig. 20C), glomelliferic acid, lobaric acid, norlobaridon, physodic acid (short curved needle clusters in G.A.W., Fig. 20D).

K—, P—, C—, KC—: Barbatic acid (prisms in G.E.), bellidiflorin, caperatic acid (feathery globules in G.E., Fig. 20E), diffractaic acid, divaricatic acid (crisscrossed needles in G.A.W., Fig. 20F), evernic acid (bushy clusters in G.E., Fig. 20G), grayanic acid (long straight needles in G.E., Fig. 20H), homosekikaic acid, lichexanthone (orange fluorescent in UV), merochlorophaeic acid (long lamellae in G.A.W. and G.E.), perlatolic acid (gummy residue, long curved needles in G.A.W.), protolichesterinic acid (feathery lamellae in G.E.), rangiformic acid, sphaerophorin, squamatic acid, tenuiorin (long curved needles in G.A.o-T.), ursolic acid, zeorin (hexagonal prisms in G.A.o-T.).

The crystal tests fail most often because (1) too much reagent is added and the coverslip floats, (2) overheating dissolves all of the residue, and (3) the residue is too small to recrystallize. Undissolved residue or sand grains are sometimes mistaken for crystals; only clean crystals free of debris should be examined.

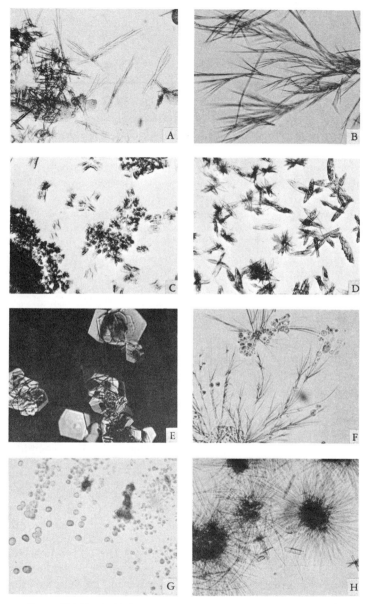

Figure 19A-H. A, Usnic acid from G.E.; B, atranorin from G.A.o-T.;
C, norstictic acid from G.A.o-T.; D, salacinic acid from G.A.o-T.; E, stictic
acid from G.A.o-T.; F, protocetraric acid (warts) with atranorin from
G.A.o-T.; G, gyrophoric acid from G.E.; and H, lecanoric acid from G.A.W.

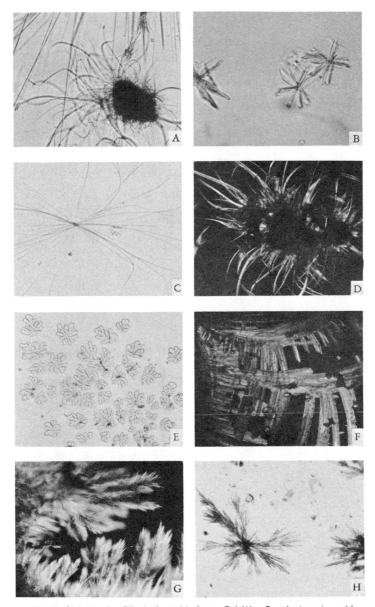

Figure 20A-H. A, Olivetoric acid from G.A.W.; B, alectoronic acid from G.A.W.; C, cryptochlorophaeic acid from G.A.W.; D, physodic acid from G.A.W.; E, caperatic acid from G.E.; F, divaricatic acid from G.A.W.; G, evernic acid from G.E.; and H, grayanic acid from G.E.

Chromatography

The crystal tests have proved to be reliable and consistent means for identifying most of the lichen substances. However, some substances form no crystals, when crystallized are not distinctive, or fail to crystallize because of interference from other substances present. These difficulties have been largely overcome with paper and thin-layer chromatography. Lichen substances can be chromatographed easily with standard one-dimensional techniques that are now commonplace in most laboratories (Fig. 21). Rather than rely on R_f values, which vary depending on solvents and tempera-

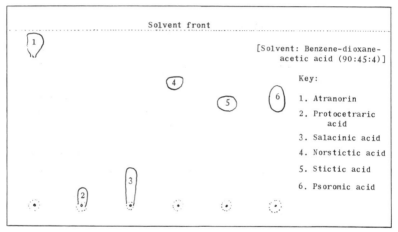

Figure 21. A tracing of a typical thin-layer chromatogram.

ture, one should always run known compounds along with the unknowns on the same chromatogram and compare the spots. It will take some practice to interpret spots on chromatograms, but by using the method of comparing spots and using different solvents, unknowns can eventually be identified with detective work.

An acetone extract of the thallus is applied to the sheet or precoated plate, blowing to keep the spot small, and the plate put in a chamber containing a solvent such as n-butanol-acetone-water (5:4:1), benzene-dioxane-formic acid (90:45:4), or any of several others. Experimentation will determine which solvent makes the best separation of spots. Colorless substances can be made visible by spraying with 5% sulfuric acid or ferric chloride. Examination under ultraviolet light can be extremely helpful.

Fluorescence Analysis

Students with access to an ultraviolet lamp, even an ordinary sun lamp with appropriate filters, will find that some lichens show brilliant fluorescence. If at all possible, every specimen collected should be examined. Bright white fluorescence is characteristic of squamatic acid, which is an important diagnostic acid in *Cladonia*. In the foliose groups alectoronic acid is highly fluorescent; divaricatic acid, evernic acid, and perlatolic acid fluoresce noticeably but with less intensity. Lichexanthone and rhizocarpic acid, both in the cortex of some lichens, turn a brilliant orange. Be extremely careful to shield your eyes from the ultraviolet rays; serious eye damage can result, even from radiation reflected from the surface of white chromatograms exposed under a UV lamp.

WHERE TO LOOK

Lichens grow on trees, dead wood, rocks, tombstones, mosses, soil, and other substrates. Each species will usually grow best on only one kind of substrate. The vast majority prefer sunny exposed habitats, but a few genera, especially those with blue-green algae (*Collema, Leptogium, Peltigera*) grow well in moist shady woods. Some species of *Dermatocarpon* and *Leptogium* may actually grow on rocks in or near running water.

Ideal collecting places for lichens are open dry oak woods and rock outcrops throughout the Appalachian Mountains, Ohio River Valley, southern United States, the northern states, and the Pacific coast region. For sheer abundance, the boreal spruce fir forests of southern Canada and adjacent United States are unrivaled. Deserts generally have mostly soil lichens, but a surprising number of other kinds may be found on scrub oaks and among boulders in the Southwest. Isolated woodlots in the heavily farmed Midwest and Prairie states are often rather poor in lichens, as are many river bottom forests. Lichens will be poorly developed or lacking in large industrial cities since most have been killed off by air pollution.

Foliose corticolous lichens and soil Cladonias will be collected frequently. Some of the most interesting species are found in the top branches and canopies, and a thorough collector will always be on the lookout for recently felled trees, especially in southern United States.

HOW TO COLLECT AND STUDY

Lichens are usually collected with a knife or hammer and chisel. The thalli are fairly firm and leathery when dry, but some species become extremely brittle and crumble easily. Since all lichens turn pliable and rubbery when moistened, it is often wise to wet the thalli before attempting to collect specimens which adhere closely to rock or bark. A specimen as large as the palm of the hand should be collected if at all possible. The important thing to remember is that the larger and more uniform a collection is the more scientific value it has. Specimens can be put in paper or cloth sacks if dry and stored indefinitely. Wet specimens should be spread out on newspaper to dry. *Never put lichens in plastic collecting bags* that are now used so often for fungi or higher plants. Moisture cannot evaporate from these bags and the lichen thalli, even if just slightly moist, will quickly discolor or mold.

Dried field collections may be sorted and curated at leisure. Small specimens on bark need only be trimmed somewhat and pasted on 3 x 4″ cards. Larger fruticose specimens ordinarily require wetting and light pressing between blotters if they are too bulky. Lichens are best dried in front of a fan with forced air; uncirculated artificial heat must be avoided because of the danger of molding. Specimens are finally placed in packets and a label attached (Fig. 22). They may be stored upright in shoe or file boxes, or the packets may be stapled or pasted on sheets of standard herbarium paper and stored in genus folders in herbarium cabinets.

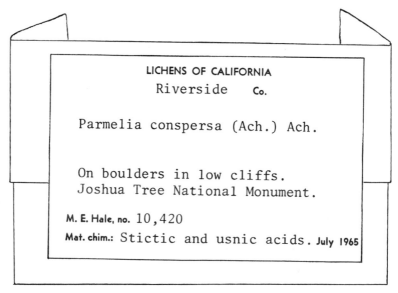

LICHENS OF CALIFORNIA
Riverside   Co.

Parmelia conspersa (Ach.) Ach.

On boulders in low cliffs.
Joshua Tree National Monument.

M. E. Hale, no. 10,420
Mat. chim.: Stictic and usnic acids. July 1965

Figure 22. Example of a folded packet with label.

As a final note, you should be sure to obtain permission before collecting lichens in State and National Parks. Do not completely collect or destroy small or rare colonies of lichens, but leave some in place in order to continue the species. Lichens grow very slowly and can be exterminated by overcollecting.

USES OF LICHENS

The main economic importance of lichens is in their use as antibiotics. In Europe yellow lichens (mostly *Cladonia*) are harvested for the extraction of usnic acid, which is the base of an effective antibiotic salve. Lichens, particularly Iceland Moss (*Cetraria islandica*), are still used as expectorants and have an important place in Chinese medicine. Desert tribes in North Africa smoke lichen mixtures.

Other lichens in Europe are extensively collected, and the essential oils they contain used as a perfume base and fixative. Some serve as a mash for making alcoholic beverages. Litmus paper, a familiar acid-base indicator in chemical laboratories, was originally made with amphoteric lichen dyes.

Lichens have some food value, according to reports as much as breakfast cereals, and can be eaten in emergencies. Rock tripes (*Umbilicaria*), for example, are boiled to extract a gelatinous soup thickener. They can also be washed with cold water to remove dirt particles and eaten directly or fried in fat. Lichens containing fumarprotocetraric acid ("Iceland Moss," many Cladonias) should be avoided because they have a bitter taste.

The Reindeer Mosses (*Cladonia rangiferina, C. evansii, etc.*) are widely employed as facsimile trees and shrubs in model train or city layouts, miniature Japanese gardens, and in floral arrangements. They are sometimes treated with glycerine to make them pliable and dyed green or red.

Rocks with attached lichens may be added to rock gardens. Some may succumb to air pollution or a change in locality, but they can add color and variety for a number of years.

PROJECTS WITH LICHENS

There are many interesting projects that can be done with lichens. If carried out with care, they can add to our scientific knowledge about lichens.

Lichens and Air Pollution

Lichens are extremely sensitive to air pollution, especially sulphur dioxide. Their absence may be used as a measure of how much a city is polluted. For example, if one methodically collects lichens in and around his own city, a map of the species distribution will show the patterns of air pollution. The sooner projects like this are started the better, for levels of pollution are rising. Re-surveys several years later can show how fast and in what direction pollution is progressing.

Lichen Dyes

Lichens were used by American Indians and are still the basis of cottage dye industries in northern Europe. Bolton's excellent little text summarizes the techniques used. Briefly, one can extract lichen dyes by boiling a panful of thalli in water for several hours, using any of the common lichens, or by treating C+ red lichens with ammonia for a week or two without heat. White wool dipped or soaked in the extracts will turn various shades of red, orange, or brown, depending on the length of time it is left in.

Culturing Lichens

Physiological studies of lichens can only be conducted if one has access to an autoclave for sterilizing glassware and media. Hale's *Lichen Handbook* or better Ahmadjian's text on symbiosis contain information on culture techniques. Spore isolation from moist apothecia is preferred with culture in test tubes (Fig. 23) or flasks. Some crustose species form good colonies in a few weeks, but others may never germinate or grow only very slowly. Presence or absence of antibiotic substances can be tested in these cultures.

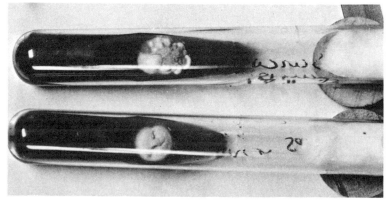

Figure 23. Test tube cultures of a lichen fungus on agar.

Lichen Growth

Lichen students interested in photography will find colorful and unusual subjects among lichens, and they can also put this hobby to scientific use by following the growth rates of lichens. Take a medium-sized foliose lichen and photograph it with a closeup lens along with a ruler. Photograph it again after a few weeks and measure how much growth has occurred (Fig. 24). Variation from month-to-month and summer-to-winter can be studied. Much work of this type remains to be done and real contributions can be made here.

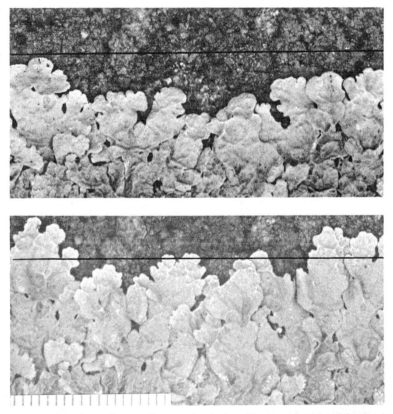

Figure 24. Comparison of the growth of *Parmelia caperata* from February to October 1968 (scale in mm).

USEFUL REFERENCES

A serious student will want to consult the references listed below, although some will be available only in university libraries. These articles treat the various species in more detail than is possible in this book and may have additional keys to forms and varieties. In particular, articles dealing with the flora of one state, as Ohio or Florida, will have shorter keys. The quarterly journal "The Bryologist" is the single most important reference for short scientific articles on lichens. One may subscribe to it at $8 per year (Department of Botany, Duke University, North Carolina 27706).

AHMADJIAN, V. 1967. The lichen symbiosis. 152 pp. Blaisdell Publ. Co., Waltham, Mass. [Excellent summary of lichen physiology and synthesis.]

BOLTON, E. M. 1960. Lichens for vegetable dyeing. 119 pp. Charles T. Branford Co., Newton Centre, Mass. [Practical guide for lichen dyeing.]

BRODO, I. M. 1968. The lichens of Long Island, New York: a vegetational and floristic analysis. New York State Museum and Science Service, Albany, New York. [Detailed treatment useful for the Northeast, including keys to both crustose and macrolichens.]

EVANS, A. W. 1943. Asahina's microchemical studies on the *Cladoniae*. Bull. Torrey Bot. Club 70:139-151. [Descriptions (but no illustrations) of crystals of the most common substances.]

FINK, B. 1935. The lichen flora of the United States. 426 pp. Univ. of Michigan Press, Ann Arbor. [Complete summary of the flora with keys and descriptions but now out of date.]

HALE, M. E. 1954. Lichens from Baffin Island. Amer. Midl. Nat. 51:236-264. [Contains keys to many arctic lichens.]

———. 1961. Lichen handbook. 178 pp. Smithsonian Institution, Washington, D.C. [General brief summary of lichenology with keys to eastern lichens.]

———. 1967. The biology of lichens. 176 pp. Ed. Arnold (Publishers), London. [College-level text on lichenology.]

LLANO, G. A. 1950. A monograph of the lichen family Umbilicariaceae in the Western Hemisphere, 281 pp. Smithsonian Institution, Washington, D.C. [Available on request to university students.]

———. 1951. Economic uses of lichens. Ann. Rep. Smithsonian Institution 1950, pp. 385-422.

MOORE, B. J. 1968. The macrolichen flora of Florida. Bryologist 71:161-265. [Complete with descriptions and keys and useful in general for the Coastal Plain from North Carolina to Texas.]

MOTYKA, J. 1964. The North American species of *Alectoria*. Bryologist 67:1-44. [Keys and descriptions.]

NEARING, G. G. 1947. The lichen book. 648 pp. Eric Lundberg, Ashton, Md. [A complete but now out of date treatment of eastern lichens with numerous small line drawings.]

SIERK, H. A. 1964. The genus *Leptogium* in North America north of Mexico. Bryologist 67:245-317. [Monographic treatment with keys and illustrations.]

TAYLOR, FR. CONAN J. 1967. The foliose and fruticose lichens of Ohio. 100 pp. Ohio Biological Survey. [Excellent and well-illustrated flora of the Ohio lichens.]

THOMSON, J. W. 1950. The species of *Peltigera* of North America north of Mexico. Amer. Midl. Nat. 44:1-68. [Monographic treatment with keys and descriptions.]

———. 1963. The lichen genus *Physcia* in North America. Beih. Nova Hedwigia 7. 172 pp. [A monographic treatment with keys, descriptions, and photographs.]

———. 1967. The lichen genus *Cladonia* in North America. 200 pp. Univ. of Toronto Press, Toronto, Canada. [Complete illustrated treatment of *Cladonia*.]

WEBER, W. A. 1963. Lichens of the Chiricahua Mountains, Arizona. Univ. Colorado Studies. Biol. No. 10. [Includes a number of valuable keys to southwestern lichens.]

WETMORE, C. M. 1960. The lichen genus *Nephroma* in North and Middle America. Michigan State Univ. Biol. Series 1:372-452. [Monographic treatment with keys and descriptions.]

———. 1968. Lichen flora of the Black Hills. Michigan State Univ. Biol. series. [A complete survey with keys and descriptions for crustose and macrolichens; no illustrations.]

HOW TO USE THE PICTURED-KEY

This key contains 357 main entries and mentions an additional 225 rarer species or chemical variants. The key is divided into five main sections, I. Stratified Foliose, II. Gelatinous, III. Umbilicate, IV. Fruticose, and V. Squamulose, and within each group the key begins with number 1. Once the correct group is chosen, test each pair of key numbers until a fit between an unknown specimen and the illustration, map, and description is reached. Geography can be a most useful character, for if a certain species falls outside of your state or area, it may usually be eliminated from consideration, although of course we should expect some range extensions.

Not every specimen can be positively identified to species, because no key can possibly include all the variations of highly plastic genera with many "hybrids," such as *Alectoria*, *Cladonia*, *Collema*, *Ramalina*, and *Usnea*. A serious beginner is best advised to request help from lichenologists at universities or museums for identification or verification. Etiquette demands that only good, well labeled specimens be sent.

A millimeter scale is usually included with each illustration. Since enlargements vary, the scale should be noted with care. If there is no scale, one may assume that the illustration is near natural size. Finally, only positive chemical color tests are indicated along with the substance causing the color.

PICTURED-KEY TO THE FOLIOSE AND FRUTICOSE LICHENS
Key to Major Groups

1a Thallus foliose; lobes flattened, with a distinct upper and lower surface. Fig. 25. 2

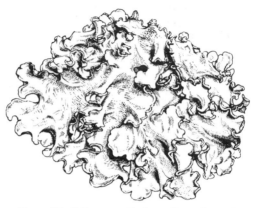

Figure 25. Foliose growth form (*Parmelia austro-sinensis*).

1b Thallus not foliose 3

2a Thallus stratified (section with a razor blade), with a white or brightly colored medulla and a thin green algal layer (use hand lens). Fig. 26. .... I. *Stratified Foliose Lichens* (p. 30)

Figure 26. Sectioning a foliose thallus to expose medulla.

2b Thallus without internal layers, the medulla dark or black. ......
....II. *Gelatinous Lichens* (p. 124)

3a Thallus umbilicate, round in outline and attached by a single cord below. Fig. 27. ....III. *Umbilicate Lichens* (p. 134)

Figure 27. Top and side view of an umbilicate lichen (*Umbilicaria mammulata*).

3b Thallus fruticose; lobes round or somewhat flattened in cross section, without a distinct upper and lower surface. Fig. 28.
....IV. *Fruticose Lichens* (p. 140)

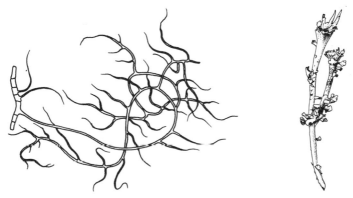

Figure 28. Fruticose growth form of *Usnea* (left) and *Cladonia*.

3c Thallus squamulose, consisting of numerous often crowded
   squamules up to 1 cm long. Fig. 29. ....
   .... V. *Squamulose Lichens* (p. 203)

Figure 29. Squamulose growth form of *Cladonia*.

I. Stratified Foliose Lichens

These are by far the most commonly collected lichens on tree
trunks and branches and on rocks. I have included here the following genera:*Anaptychia, Anzia, Candelaria, Cetraria, Cetrelia,
Coccocarpia, Dermatocarpon, Dirinaria, Hypogymnia, Lobaria,
Menegazzia, Nephroma, Pannaria, Parmelia, Parmeliella, Parmeliopsis, Peltigera, Physcia, Platismatia, Pseudocyphellaria, Pyxine,
Solorina, Sticta,* and *Xanthoria,* as well as lobate species of the
crustose *Caloplaca, Lecanora,* and *Rinodina.* These genera are separated by spore and vegetative characters, but since so many specimens are sterile, a key to genera is impractical. I have used three
main artificial divisions, sorediate species, isidiate species, and those
without soredia or isidia, and under these, thallus color, width of
lobes, color of lower surface, presence of cilia, pseudocyphellae,
etc. are used to separate species. Three genera, however, are so
unusual that they are keyed out first: *Peltigera* with veins below,
Pseudocyphellaria with white or yellow pores on the lower surface,
and *Sticta* with large recessed pores on the lower surface.

1a Lower surface with veins (do not use hand lens); thallus usually
   collected on soil or mosses. Fig. 30. *Peltigera.* 4

1b Lower surface without veins. 2

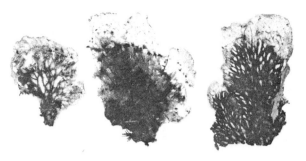

Figure 30. Examples of veins in *Peltigera* species (X1).

2a Lower surface with pores (do not use hand lens). Fig. 31.
    Pseudocyphellaria and *Sticta*..12 (p. 36)

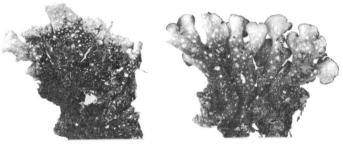

Figure 31. Pores on the lower surface of *Pseuaocyphellaria* (left) and *Sticta* (X1).

2b Lower surface without pores. 3
3a Thallus sorediate. Fig. 32. ....16 (p. 39)
3b Thallus isidiate. Fig. 32. ....92 (p. 71)
3c Thallus without soredia or isidia. ....136 (p. 87)

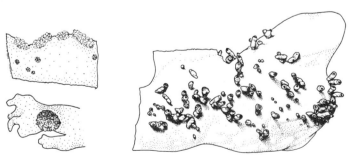

Figure 32. Comparison of soredia (left) and isidia (X10).

4a Upper surface of lobes with small dark green warts (cephalodia); thallus turning bright green when moistened. Fig. 33. ....
....*Peltigera aphthosa* (**L.**) **Willd.**

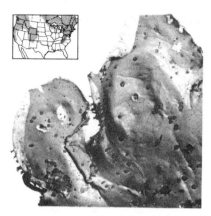

Figure 33.

Thallus pale smoke gray to tea green (when dry), loosely adnate to suberect on soil and over mosses, 10-20 cm broad; lower surface light drab, the veins pale or indistinct; apothecia common, erect. Common and conspicuous i n the boreal forests but becoming rarer southward in the United States. Identification in the field is easy once the cephalodia are recognized.

4b Warts lacking on the upper surface; thallus not turning green when wet. 5

5a Thallus with laminal or marginal soredia 6

5b Thallus lacking soredia. 7

6a Soredia laminal in orbicular soralia. Fig. 34. ....
....*Peltigera spuria* (**Ach.**) **DC.**

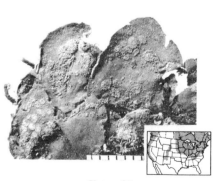

Figure 34.

Thallus brownish gray, adnate, 3-7 cm broad; upper surface finely tomentose; lower surface light tan, the veins raised, pale or brownish, rhizines distinct; apothecia very rare. Scattered on soil in woods or along roadbanks but often overlooked. This species is quite evanescent and colonies can disappear in a year. It is related to *P. canina* and may only be a transitional growth form.

6b Soralia marginal, linear. Fig. 35. .... *Peltigera collina* (Ach.) Ach.

Thallus greenish or brownish gray, 5-10 cm broad; upper surface becoming scabrid near the tips; margins curled upward, densely sorediate; lower surface tan, the veins flattened and indistinct, darkening, rhizines sparse; apothecia not common, erect. Widespread on soil and over mosses in western North America. It is not easily confused with any other species.

Figure 35.

7a Thallus isidiate or with tiny dense squamules. 8

7b Thallus lacking isidia or well-developed squamules. 9

8a Isidia round, mostly laminal. Fig. 36. ....
....*Peltigera evansiana* **Gyel.**

Thallus light brown, adnate, 6-12 cm broad; isidia short and globular; lower surface pale, the veins distinct, rhizines usually well developed; apothecia very rare. Common on soil in fairly closed woods and on sheltered roadbanks. The isidia distinguish this rather rare species from *P. canina.* In western North America, especially in Colorado, and rarely eastward, one will find another isidiate species, *P. lepidophora* (Nyl.) Vain. It has peculiar peltate isidia.

Figure 36.

8b Isidia squamulose, flattened, mostly marginal or along cracks in the cortex. Fig. 37. ....*Peltigera praetextata* (Somm.) Vain.

Thallus whitish to brownish gray, loosely adnate, 5-15 cm broad; upper surface densely tomentose; lower surface buff to cream, the veins pale, raised, the rhizines conspicuous; apothecia very rare, erect. Less common than *P. canina* and intergrading with it. Another squamulate species, *P. elizabethae* Gyel., differs in having a shiny upper cortex and dark flattened veins.

Figure 37.

9a Lower surface with pale narrow raised veins; rhizines conspicuous. Fig. 38. Dog Lichen ....*Peltigera canina* (L.) Willd.

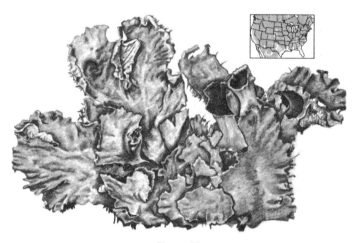

Figure 38.

Thallus light brown with a whitish cast when dry, deeper brown when wet, adnate on soil, humus, or mosses, 6-20 cm broad; lower surface tan to whitish, without a cortex, the veins raised, the same color or darkening, rhizines pale, tufted and conspicuous; apothecia common, erect. Extremely widespread throughout most of North America. This lichen is highly variable. A darker brown sun-form with smaller curled lobes is sometimes recognized as *P. rufescens* (Weiss) Humb., but it is difficult to separate them. *P. degeni* Gyel., which occurs from New England to South Dakota, has similar raised veins but a shiny cortex without tomentum (as in *P. poly-dactyla*). *P. membranacea* (Ach.) Nyl. in northern areas has very broad lobes and a thin thallus and is probably a good species.

9b Lower surface with dark flattened veins or veins not clearly distinguishable; rhizines inconspicuous. **10**

10a Thallus small, 1-2 cm broad, fan-shaped. Fig. 39. Fan Lichen. ....*Peltigera venosa* (**L.**) **Baumg.**

Thallus light brown, adnate to sub-erect on soil, composed of separate lobes; upper surface shiny and smooth; lower surface with dark veins sparsely covered with tiny greenish warts (cephalodia); rhizines inconspicuous; apothecia common, horizontal. Rather rare except in boreal areas and easily overlooked because of the small size.

Figure 39.

10b Thallus larger, 6-20 cm broad with long lobes. **11**

11a Apothecia lacking or if present erect. Fig. 40. ....
....*Peltigera polydactyla* (**Neck.**) **Hoffm.**

Thallus brownish gray; upper surface shiny; lower surface buff, the veins darkening; apothecia common, erect. Very common in open forests and on sheltered roadbanks. *Peltigera elizabethae* has identical lower surface but with dense marginal squamules and granules. In boreal regions of Canada and western United States one may find *P. scabrosa* Th. Fr. which has a dull scabrid cortex. *P. mala-cea* (Ach.) Funck, another arctic-boreal species, has a greenish color, pubescent lobe tips, and very thick tomentum with veins barely distinguishable.

Figure 40.

11b Apothecia always present, horizontal. Fig. 41. ....
.... *Peltigera horizontalis* (Huds.) Baumg.

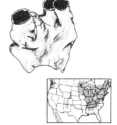

Thallus brownish mineral gray, loosely adnate, 6-12 cm broad; upper surface shiny; lower surface buff, the veins flattened, rhizines sparse. Fairly common in moist woods. This species is separated from *P. polydactyla* chiefly by the horizontal apothecia. Sterile specimens of *P. horizontalis* would therefore be identified as *P. polydactyla*.

Figure 41.

12a Pores recessed (cyphellae). Fig. 42. 13

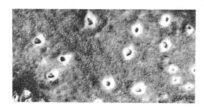

Figure 42. Recessed pores (cyphellae)' of *Sticta* (X10).

12b Pores not recessed (pseudocyphellae). 15

13a Upper surface isidiate. Fig. 43. ......

.... *Sticta fuliginosa* (Dicks.) Ach.

Thallus greenish to dark brown, thin, loosely attached, 5-10 cm broad; isidia usually clumped; lower surface tan, long-tomentose, with inconspicuous cyphellae; apothecia lacking. Rare on tree bases and mosses at higher elevations. The commoner *S. weigelii* is more leathery and has marginal soredia.

Figure 43.

13b Margins and in part upper surface sorediate or sorediate-isidiate. 14

14a Soredia granular to subisidiate, marginal. Fig. 44. ....
....Sticta weigelii (Ach.) Vain.

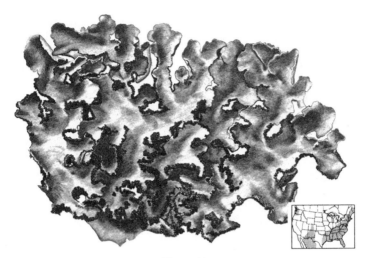

Figure 44.

Thallus brown to drab, loosely attached, 4-15 cm broad; lower surface light brown, tomentum dense; apothecia rare. Base of trees and on rocks in open woods, most common in the South. The cyphellae are conspicuous and make identification easy. Some specimens in the Western States may have coarse, mostly laminal isidia; these appear to be S. sylvatica (Huds.) Ach., a European species.

14b Soredia powdery, laminal and in part marginal. Fig. 45. ....
....Sticta limbata (Sm.) Ach.

Thallus light brown, loosely attached, 4-10 cm broad; upper surface
plane to somewhat ridged; lower surface buff, short-tomentose, cyphellae
inconspicuous; apothecia lacking. Fairly common on bark or over mosses on
the Pacific Coast.

Figure 45.

15a Pores and exposed soredia yellow. Fig. 46. ....
....*Pseudocyphellaria aurata* (**Ach.**) **Vain.**

Figure 46.

Thallus buffy olive, turning green when wet, loosely adnate, 4-10 cm broad; soredia marginal; lower surface pale tan, short tomentose; apothecia very rare. Conspicuous but not often collected, on trees in open deciduous forests. Closely related *P. crocata* (L.) Vain. has numerous small laminal soralia and occurs at higher elevations in the Appalachians, northern Great Lakes region, and the Pacific Northwest. Older books will list the *Pseudocyphellaria* species under *Sticta* but the pores are different.

15b Pores and soredia (if present) white. Fig. 47. ....
....*Pseudocyphellaria anthraspis* (**Ach.**) **Magn.**

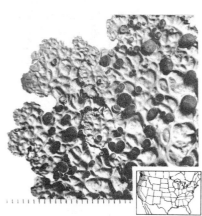

Figure 47.

Thallus brown to light brown, leathery, loosely attached, 6-20 cm broad; upper surface strongly ridged (without lens), shiny, without soredia; lower surface tan, short tomentose with numerous pores; apothecia common. On bark or rocks in open woods, often on dead conifer branches. Superficially it resembles *Lobaria pulmonaria* or *L. linita*, but these species have a mottled lower surface without pores. A sorediate form, often intermixed, is called *P. anomola* Magn. A fourth species in the genus, *P. rainerensis* Imsh. from Mt. Rainer, Washington, has large fragile lobes and marginal lobules.

SOREDIATE FOLIOSE LICHENS (Fig. 48)

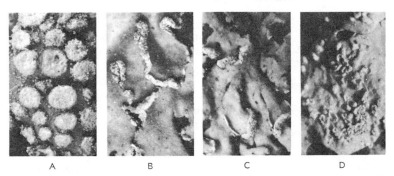

Figure 48. Types of soralia. A, laminal; B, marginal; C, apical; D, pustular (all X5-10).

16a Thallus orange; cortex K+ deep purple. 17

16b Thallus not orange; cortex K— or K+ yellowish. 19

17a Thallus crustose at the center, always growing on rocks; lower cortex and rhizines lacking (with hand lens). Fig. 49. ....
.... *Caloplaca sorediata* (Vain.) DR.

Thallus deep ochraceous orange, appressed, 2-4 cm broad but often fusing into larger colonies; upper surface coarsely sorediate to sorediate-isidiate; lower surface white; apothecia lacking. Widespread on exposed rocks, especially along lake or ocean fronts. *Xanthoria candelaria,* which may be intermingled, is distinctly foliose with scattered soredia.

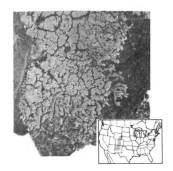

Figure 49.

17b Thallus foliose (though often very small), growing on tree bark or more rarely on rocks; lower cortex and rhizines present (under lens). 18

18a Lobes rather coarse, averaging 1 mm wide, little branched;
soredia marginal and under lobe tips. Fig. 50. ....
....*Xanthoria fallax* (**Hepp**) **Arn.**

Thallus deep orange on exposed trees
to pale greenish yellow on shaded
trunks, closely adnate, 2-4 cm broad
but often fusing into broad colonies;
lower surface white; apothecia not
common. Widespread and commonly
collected on oaks, aspen, and roadside
elm trees. The lobes are quite coarse
and unbranched when compared with
those of typical *X. candelaria,* with
which it intergrades.

Figure 50. Thallus showing
soralia (X4).

18b Lobes finely divided, 0.2-0.5 mm wide; soredia scattered,
mostly apical or laminal. Fig. 51. ....
....*Xanthoria candelaria* (**L.**) **Th. Fr.**

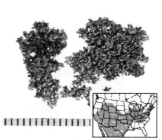

Thallus ochraceous orange, closely adnate, 2-4 cm broad; lower surface white;
apothecia rare. Widespread on deciduous
trees in open woods and along roadsides,
more rarely on rocks. It may be difficult
to separate from *X. fallax.* The main differences are lobe width and position of
soredia. *X. candelaria* is apparently the
more common of the two in arctic and
western North America. *Candelaria concolor* is very similar in morphology but
has a yellow color and K— reaction.

Figure 51.

19a Thallus pale lemon yellow, light green or greenish yellow. 20

19b Thallus not yellow or green (when dry). 28

20a Lobes quite broad and apically rotund, 3-10 mm wide. 21

20b Lobes narrow, 0.1-3.0 mm wide. 23

21a Upper cortex with white pores (look toward lobe tips with low
    power lens). Fig. 52. ....*Parmelia flaventior* **Stirt.**

Thallus greenish yellow, loosely attached, 5-10 cm broad; soredia mostly laminal but also
marginal; lower surface black
with a broad naked brown zone
along the margins; apothecia
very rare. Medulla C+, KC+
red (lecanoric acid). Common
on trees in open woods or along
roadsides. This lichen has been
confused with *P. caperata,* which
differs in lacking pores and in
having a C−, P+ red medullary
reaction as well as laminal pustular soredia. *P. ulophyllodes* is
very close but lacks white pores.

Figure 52.

21b Upper cortex continuous, without white pores. 22

22a Soredia marginal in crescent-shaped soralia, powdery. Fig. 53.
    ....*Parmelia ulophyllodes* **(Vain.) Sav.**

Thallus yellowish green, adnate, 4-8
cm broad; upper surface rather wrinkled; sorediate lobes in part suberect;
lower surface black or dark brown,
naked and lighter brown near the margins; apothecia very rare. Medulla C+,
KC+ red (lecanoric acid). On conifers
and deciduous trees in open woods.
This species intergrades with *P. flaventior* extensively in western states and
it may be difficult to make firm determinations.

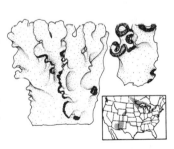

Figure 53.

22b Soredia laminal, often diffuse and granular or pustulate. Fig.
    54. ....*Parmelia caperata* **(L.) Ach.**

Thallus pale yellowish green, adnate, 5-20 cm broad and often
covering large areas; upper surface becoming much wrinkled,
faintly white-reticulate (under lens) at lobe tips; lower surface
black with a narrow marginal bare zone; apothecia rare. Medulla

P+ brick red (protocetraric acid). Very common on trees in open woods and along roadsides and on rocks. The resemblance to *P. flaventior* is discussed above. If growing on rock, it should be carefully distinguished from *P. conspersa,* which has cylindrical isidia.

Figure 54. *Parmelia caperata.*

23a Lobes finely branched, 0.1-0.3 mm wide, soredia scattered. Fig. 55. ....*Candelaria concolor* **(Dicks.) Stein.**

Figure 55.

Thallus greenish lemon yellow, closely adnate, 0.2-1.0 cm broad but fusing into larger colonies; lower surface white, rhizinate; apothecia rare. Common on ash, elm, and sugar maple in open woods. Variety *effusa* of this species has no distinct lobes but only masses of yellow soredia. Both react K− in contrast to the K+ purple of *Xanthoria candelaria.*

25a Medulla deep lemon yellow (expose with razor blade). Fig. 56
.... *Cetraria pinastri* (Scop.) S. Gray

Thallus light yellow green, adnate, 1-2 cm broad; lower surface white, sparsely rhizinate; apothecia very rare. Common and conspicuous at the base of trees and rocks in the boreal forests. This brilliant species often occurs with *Parmeliopsis ambigua*.

Figure 56.

25b Medulla white. Fig. 57. .... *Cetraria oakesiana* **Tuck.**

Thallus yellowish green, adnate, 3-7 cm broad, the lobes often more or less parallel; lower surface light tan to white, sparsely rhizinate; apothecia rare; erect black marginal pycnidia sometimes present. Common on the bark of conifers and hardwoods and on rocks in northern woods. Forms of *P. ulophyllodes* with a pale lower surface may key out here, but they have broader lobes and a C+ red reaction in the medulla.

Figure 57.

26a Lobes 0.5-1.0 mm wide; rhizines simple, sparse. 27

26b Lobes 1-2 mm wide; rhizines dense, branched (under low power lens). Fig. 58. .... *Parmelia sinuosa* (Sm.) **Ach.**

Thallus greenish yellow, loosely adnate; 2-6 cm broad; soralia mostly subterminal; lower surface black; apothecia lacking. Medulla K+ yellow→red, P | pale orange (salacinic acid). Rare on trees in open woods from coastal Oregon northward into Canada.

Figure 58.

27a Collected in northern and western states and Canada. Fig. 59.
....*Parmeliopsis ambigua* **(Wulf.) Nyl.**

Figure 59.

Thallus greenish yellow, closely adnate, 2-4 cm broad; soredia in powdery capitate soralia, often becoming very dense; lower surface black to dark brown, rarely tan; apothecia rare. Widespread on conifers and deciduous trees, rarely on rocks. *Parmeliopsis hyperopta* is the gray acid-deficient counterpart and the two often occur together. *P. halei* (below) has pustular soredia and a different range. A rare species in Colorado, *P. mougeotii* Pers., grows on rocks and externally is very close but contains stictic acid (K+ yellow).

27b Collected in the Piedmont and Coastal Plain of southeastern United States. Fig. 60. ....*Parmeliopsis halei* **(Tuck.) Hale**

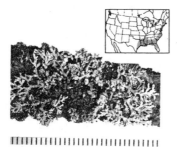

Figure 60.

Thallus greenish yellow, closely adnate, 2-4 cm broad; upper surface pustulate and diffusely sorediate; lower surface uniformly whitish to cream; apothecia rare. Common on pine trees and burned stumps in open woods and along roadsides. This species was formerly identified with *P. ambigua.*

28a Thallus coffee or chestnut brown. 29

28b Thallus not brown. 35

29a Soredia diffuse, in part isidiate, leaving a whitish cast when rubbed with fingers. Fig. 61. ....*Parmelia subaurifera* **Nyl.**

Thallus brown, adnate, 4-8 cm broad;
lower surface light brown, rarely blackening, moderately rhizinate; apothecia
rare. Medulla C+, KC+ red (lecanoric
acid). Very common on deciduous trees
and conifers in open woods and along
roadsides. This is the most common
brown *Parmelia* in eastern North America. The only similar species is *P.
subargentifera* (below), which has
marginal soredia and a jet black lower
surface.

Figure 61.

29b Soredia delimited in linear or orbicular soralia. 30

30a Upper cortex rough and white pruinose (under lens, see Fig.
     5D); thallus turning green when wet. ....
     ....*Physcia grisea* (see p. 56)

30b Upper cortex smooth, not pruinose; thallus not turning green
     when wet. 31

31a Lobes narrow and linear, 0.5-2.0 mm wide. 32

31b Lobes broader, 2-5 mm wide. 33

32a Upper surface with tiny white pores (use high power lens);
     medulla C+ red. Fig. 62. ....*Parmelia substygia* Räs.

Thallus dark brown, closely adnate,
3-8 cm broad; upper surface shiny;
lower surface sparsely rhizinate, black;
apothecia rare. Medulla C+, KC+ red
(gyrophoric acid). Widespread on
boulders, rarely on wood, in open
areas. A few reports of this species in
eastern North America have been con-
firmed. The diagnostic character is the
white pores.

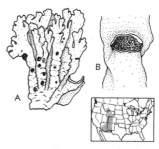

Figure 62. A, thallus (X2);
B, soralium (X8).

32b Upper surface continuous, pores lacking; medulla C—. Fig. 63.
....*Parmelia sorediosa* **Almb.**

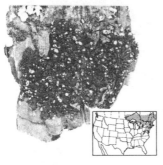

Figure 63.

Thallus dark brown, closely adnate, 2-5 cm broad; lower surface brown to blackish, sparsely rhizinate; apothecia lacking. Rare on exposed rocks in talus slopes, sometimes on dead bark. The soredia are often white and prominent but may darken. Other very similar brown species are known in western North America but their taxonomy is poorly known. *P. disjuncta* Erichs. has brownish soredia and thicker lobes. *P. loxodes* Nyl. is KC+ red (glomelliferic acid).

33a Lower surface black (turning brown only along the margins); rhizines present. Fig. 64. ....*Parmelia subargentifera* **Nyl.**

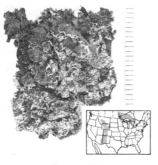

Figure 64.

Thallus chestnut to olive brown, adnate, 6-12 cm broad; soralia marginal and in part laminal; apothecia rare. Medulla C+, KC+ red (lecanoric acid). Rather common on trees in open woods and swamps, less so on rocks. It is much rarer than *P. subaurifera* but can be recognized by the different soralia and the black lower surface. In similar habitats in the western States one may find *Parmelia stictica* (Del.) Nyl., which has laminal soredia and pseudocyphellae much as in *P. subrudecta* but with a black lower surface.

33b Lower surface uniformly tan or brown; rhizines sparse or lacking. 34

34a Thallus suberect, collected on branches and upper trunk of conifers. Fig. 65. ....*Cetraria chlorophylla* (**Willd.**) **Vain.**

Figure 65.

Thallus light brown to brown, 4-8 cm broad; lower surface brown, shiny, sparsely rhizinate; apothecia lacking. Common on conifers and fenceposts. This species is very close to *Cetraria ciliaris* except for the marginal soredia.

34b Thallus adnate, collected on tree bases or rocks. Fig. 66. ....
....*Nephroma parile* (Ach.) Ach.

   Thallus light brown to brown, loosely
adnate, 4-10 cm broad; lower surface
buff, dull, naked or with very short
tomentum; apothecia rare. Base of trees
and mossy rocks in sheltered woods.
One could mistake this lichen for *Parmelia subargentifera* (above), which
has a black lower surface and rhizines.

Figure 66.

35a Lobes narrow, 0.1-3.0 mm wide, linear. Fig. 67A, B. 36
35b Lobes broader, 4-20 mm wide. Fig. 67C. ....71 (p. 62)
36a Lobes finely branched, 0.1-0.5 mm wide (Fig. 67A) 37

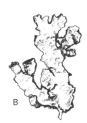

Figure 67. Lobe widths (X1). A, narrow and dissected; B.
narrow and linear; C, broad and rotund.

**36b Lobes not finely branched, broader, more than 0.5 mm
       wide.** 38
**37a Collected on trees (rarely on rocks); lobes 0.2-0.5 mm wide.
       Fig. 68.** ....*Physcia millegrana* **Degel.**

   Thallus whitish mineral gray, adnate
to closely attached, 1-2 cm broad but
fusing into larger colonies; lower surface white, sparsely rhizinate; apothecia
sometimes present. Cortex K+ yellow
(atranorin). Very common on roadside
trees and in open woods and rarely
also on rocks. Specimens from California were probably introduced on nurs-
ery tree stock from the East.

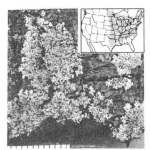

Figure 68.

37b Always collected on rocks; lobes 0.1-0.3 mm wide. Fig. 69.
.... *Physcia subtilis* Degel.

Thallus whitish mineral gray, closely adnate, 0.5-1.0 cm broad, often coalescing into larger colonies; lower surface white, sparsely rhizinate; apothecia rare. Cortex and medulla K+ yellow (atranorin). Widespread on exposed granitic boulders or sandstone. *Physcia halei* is similar but lacks soredia.

Figure 69.

38a Lower surface uniformly white to tan or light brown (under low power lens if necessary) (orange in *Anaptychia obscurata*).
....39

38b Lower surface black (sometimes brown in a narrow zone along the margin) (difficult to determine in tightly adnate species of *Dirinaria* and *Placopsis gelida*). 48

39a Soredia mostly laminal in orbicular soralia. 40

39b Soredia mostly marginal or apical (if apical on the upper or lower surface). 42

40a Collected on rocks (rarely on bark); upper cortex white-spotted (under hand lens). Fig. 70. ......*Physcia caesia* (Hoffm.) Hampe

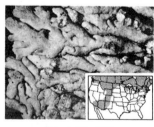

Thallus whitish mineral gray, closely adnate, 4-8 cm broad; lower surface white to buff, moderately rhizinate; apothecia rare. Cortex and medulla K+ yellow (atranorin). Widespread on boulders and cliffs in open woods or exposed areas.

Figure 70. (X3)

40b Collected on bark; white spots lacking. 41

41a Collected in the eastern deciduous forest; medulla K+ yellow. Fig. 71. .... *Physcia tribacoides* **Nyl.**

Thallus whitish mineral gray, adnate, 1.5-3.0 cm broad; lower surface white, moderately rhizinate; apothecia rare. Cortex and medulla K+ yellow (atranorin). Common in open deciduous forests, especially on white oak. In California this species is replaced by *P. clementi* (Sm.) Lynge, which has more diffuse soralia.

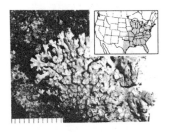

Figure 71.

41b Collected in the northern and western states and Canada; medulla K—. ....*Parmeliopsis hyperopta* (**Ach.**) **Arn.**

Thallus the same as *Parmeliopsis ambigua* (see p. 44) except whitish mineral gray. Cortex K+ yellow (atranorin). These two species have the same geographic range and often occur together at the base of trees, on stumps, and on twigs of conifers.

42a Soredia marginal and apical. Fig. 72. ....*Anaptychia ravenelii* (**Tuck.**) **Zahlbr.**

Thallus light mineral gray, adnate, 4-6 cm broad; margins with some short projecting rhizines; lower surface white to buff, moderately rhizinate; apothecia rare. Cortex K+ yellow (atranorin); medulla K+ yellow→red, P+ pale orange (salacinic acid). Fairly common on roadside trees and in open woods. *Anaptychia speciosa* has mostly apical soredia. Another confusable species, *Physcia albicans,* has a grey lower surface.

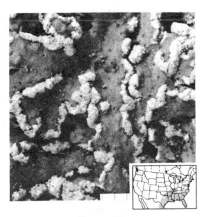

Figure 72.

42b Soredia in apical, often crescent-shaped soralia. 43

43a Tips of lobes inflated and hood-shaped (without lens). Fig. 73.
....*Physcia adscendens* **Bitt.**

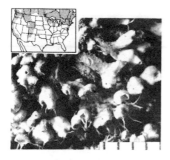

Thallus light mineral gray, adnate, 2-4 cm broad; soredia under the lobe tips; marginal cilia conspicuous; lower surface white, moderately rhizinate; apothecia very rare. Cortex K+ yellow (atranorin). Common on deciduous trees and conifers in exposed areas and along roadsides. This unusual lichen is characterized by the hood-shaped lobe tips. *Physcia tenella* (Scop.) DC., a related ciliate species, has flattened lobe tips, sorediate beneath. It is rare in North America.

Figure 73.

43b Tips of lobes plane, not hood-shaped. **44**

44a Lobe margins with long cilia, 1-4 mm long (without lens); thallus subfruticose with soredia on the lower surface. Fig. 74.
....*Anaptychia leucomelaena* **(L.) Mass.**

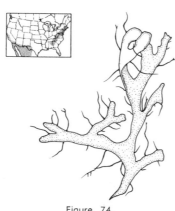

Thallus light mineral gray, loosely attached, 2-8 cm broad; lower surface white and cottony, cortex lacking; apothecia rare. Upper cortex K+ yellow (atranorin); medulla K+ yellow→red, P+ pale orange (salacinic acid). Rather rare on deciduous trees in open woods. *A. appalachensis* Kurok. is almost equally common in the Appalachian Mountains; it is K− in the medulla and has a pale yellow lower surface.

Figure 74.

44b Cilia lacking (do not confuse with projecting rhizines under low power lens). **45**

45a Soredia in apical crescent-shaped soralia; usually collected on bark but sometimes on rocks. **46**

45b Soredia in roundish to crescent-shaped soralia on the under
   side of lobe tips (under low power lens); usually collected on
   rocks. **47**

46a Lower surface orange (without lens), K+ purple. Fig. 75. ......
   .... *Anaptychia obscurata* (Nyl.) Vain.

Thallus light mineral gray,
adnate, 3-8 cm broad; lower
surface orange and cottony,
cortex lacking; rhizines marginal; apothecia very rare. Cortex K+ yellow (atranorin).
Common on deciduous trees,
more rarely on rocks, in open
woods and along roadsides. It
is very close to *A. speciosa*
(below), which is white below.
A. casarettiana Mass. has a
purplish lower cortex reacting
K— but is otherwise also very
close.

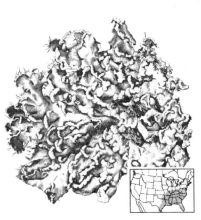

Figure 75.

46b Lower surface white (blackish in *Anaptychia casarettiana*),
   K—. Fig. 76. .... *Anaptychia speciosa* (Wulf.) Mass.

Thallus light mineral gray,
adnate, 2-8 cm broad; marginal
rhizines conspicuous; lower surface corticate, sparsely rhizinate, but the cortex often
disappearing; apothecia rare.
Cortex K+ yellow (atranorin).
Common on deciduous trees
and on mossy rocks in mature
woods and swamps. A scarcely
distinguishable chemical variant is K+ red (norstictic acid).
A. ravenelii has mostly marginal soralia and reacts K+
red. Rarer *A. casarettiana* has
a robust thallus and blackish
lower surface; it occurs mostly
in southern United States.

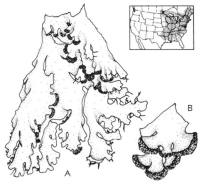

Figure 76. A, thallus (X2); B, soralia
(X4).

47a Medulla K—; eastern, boreal, and western North America. Fig. 77. ....*Physcia dubia* **(Hoffm.) Lett.**

Figure 77.

Thallus whitish mineral gray, closely adnate, 2-5 cm broad; lobes 0.5-1.0 mm wide; lower surface white to buff, moderately rhizinate; sorediate lobe tips often turning up; apothecia rare. Cortex K+ yellow (atranorin). Rather rare on exposed outcrops, sometimes on bark or wood. Another species in this difficult complex is *P. teretiuscula* (Ach.) Lynge, which differs chiefly in having narrower lobes (0.2-0.5 mm).

47b Medulla K+ yellow; western states only. Fig. 78. ....
....*Physcia callosa* **Nyl.**

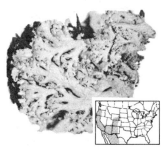

Figure 78.

Thallus whitish mineral gray, adnate, 2-6 cm broad, the colonies often coalescing; lobe margins becoming finely dissected with scattered soredia; lower surface white, moderately rhizinate; apothecia rare. Cortex and medulla K+ yellow (atranorin). Common on open rock outcrops. There may be some confusion with *P. dubia* which reacts K— in the medulla.

48a Lobes flat, solid. **50**

48b Lobes inflated, roundish, and hollow (section with razor blade). (Fig. 79). ...., ...**49**

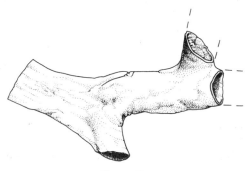

Figure 79.

49a Soredia at the tips of lobes; upper cortex continuous or with a few irregular holes. Fig. 80. ....
....*Hypogymnia physodes* **(L.) Nyl.**

Figure 80.

Thallus light mineral gray, adnate to loosely attached, 6-12 cm broad; lobes appearing inflated; soralia more or less labriform; lower surface smooth to wrinkled and irregularly lacerated and perforated; apothecia very rare. Cortex K+ yellow (atranorin); medulla KC+, P+ red (physodic acid and physodalic acid). Very common on conifers, hardwoods, and fenceposts throughout the northern forests. Two unrelated species react P—: *H. tubulosa* (Schaer.) Hav., which has distinctly elongate lobes with soralia in a ring at lobe tips, occurring with *H. physodes* but much rarer; and *H. vittata* (Ach.) Gas., which has sparse apical soralia and rather elongate lobes. In arctic-alpine regions one may find *H. austerodes* (Nyl.) Räs., which has mostly laminal soredia and a distinct brownish tinge. *Cavernularia hultenii* Degel., though flatter, has deep pores over the lower surface that make the thallus seem hollow. This is a rare conifer lichen in the Pacific Northwest and in Nova Scotia.

49b Soredia laminal; upper cortex with regular round holes. Fig. 81. ....*Menegazzia terebrata* **(Hoffm.) Mass.**

Figure 81 (X2).

Thallus light mineral gray, adnate, 6-15 cm broad; soredia powdery, often originating around the holes; lower surface deeply wrinkled, tearing away when thallus is removed from bark; apothecia very rare. Cortex K+ yellow (atranorin); medulla K+ yellow, P+ pale orange (stictic acid). Relatively rare on roadside trees and in swamps and bogs. This remarkable lichen was formerly known as *Parmelia pertusa.*

50a Medulla salmon orange or yellow (K— or K+ yellow) (use razor blade). **51**

50b Medulla white (except orange-red and K+ purple in some forms of *Physcia orbicularis*). **53**

51a Soredia in large diffuse soralia; lobes irregular, 2-5 mm wide.
.................................Parmelia aurulenta   Tuck. (see p. 57)

51b Soredia in distinct laminal or marginal soralia; lobes narrower,
1-2 mm wide, linear. 52

52a Soredia marginal and in part laminal; edges of lobes white,
split. Fig. 82. ....Pyxine sorediata (Ach.) Mont.

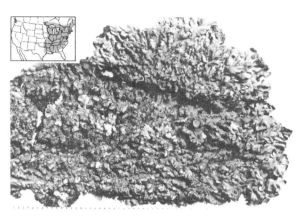

Figure 82.

Thallus whitish to greenish mineral gray, closely adnate, 3-8 cm broad; upper surface becoming scabrid or lightly pruinose; lower surface black, densely rhizinate; apothecia very rare. Medulla K+, C+, KC+ deeper yellow (unknowns). Common on deciduous trees in open forests and along roadsides.

52b Soredia all laminal or in part marginal; edges of lobes not white or split. Fig. 83. ...... Pyxine caesiopruinosa (Nyl.) Imsh.

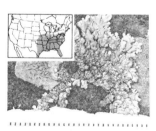

Figure 83.

Thallus whitish mineral gray, closely adnate, 2-3 cm broad; lobe tips often with a distinct patch of white pruina (under lens); lower surface black and sparsely rhizinate; apothecia very rare. Cortex brilliant orange in UV light (lichexanthone); medulla K+, C+, KC+ yellow (unknowns). Common on deciduous trees in pastures and along roadsides. Formerly confused with P. sorediata, it has mostly laminal round soralia and different chemistry. From Texas to Florida it intergrades with *P. eschweileri* (Tuck.) Vain., which lacks pruina and lichexanthone and has a finely reticulated cortex. See Imshaug's monograph (1957) for further clarification.

53a Upper surface weakly reticulately ridged and with white angular markings (see Fig. 5B) (examine lobe tips under low power lens). **54**

53b Upper surface smooth to wrinkled, without white markings. 55

54a Soralia laminal and marginal along ridges. Fig. 84. ....
....*Parmelia sulcata* **Tayl.**

Thallus whitish mineral gray, adnate, 3-10 cm broad; lower surface black and densely rhizinate, the rhizines simple or squarrosely branched (under lens); apothecia not common. Cortex K+ yellow (atranorin); medulla K+ yellow→red, P+ orange (salacinic acid). Very common on trees and rocks along roadsides or in woods. *Parmelia saxatilis* should be carefully distinguished by the coarse isidia.

Figure 84.

54b Soralia marginal. Fig. 85. ....*Parmelia fraudans* **Nyl.**

Thallus whitish mineral gray, adnate, 3-10 cm broad; lower surface black and densely rhizinate; apothecia lacking. Cortex K+ yellow (atranorin); medulla K+ yellow→red, P+ orange (salacinic acid). Common on exposed rocks near lakeshores but rarer inland. The weaker white markings and entirely marginal soralia separate this lichen from the much more common *P. sulcata*.

Figure 85.

55a Soralia mostly marginal and linear (sometimes in part laminal) (Fig. 86A). **56**

55b Soralia mostly laminal or apical, round (Fig. 86B). 59

Figure 86.

56a Collected on trees; lobes more than 1 mm wide. 57
56b Collected on rocks; lobes less than 1 mm wide. Fig. 87. ....
....*Physcia sciastra* (Ach.) DR.

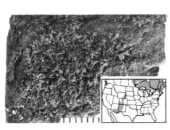

Figure 87.

Thallus blackish brown to brownish mineral gray, 2-5 cm broad; upper surface sometimes lightly pruinose; soredia becoming subisidiate; lower surface black, rhizines simple; apothecia rare. Widespread on exposed rocks, especially near lakeshores, but often overlooked because of the small size. Because of the close adnation it is hard to collect.

57a Lobes narrow and linear, 1-2 mm wide. 58
57b Lobes broader and irregular, 2-6 mm wide. ....
.. .. *Parmelia praesorediosa* Nyl. (see p. 70)
58a Upper surface scabrid and pruinose (under low power lens; see Fig. 5D); cortex and medulla K−. Fig. 88. ....
....*Physcia grisea* (Lam.) Zahlbr.

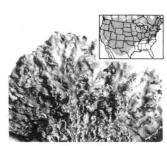

Figure 88.

Thallus greenish brown to whitish, turning green when wet, adnate, 2-6 cm broad; soredia coarse, sometimes appearing greenish; lower surface black, rarely brown, sparsely to densely rhizinate; apothecia not common. Widespread and frequently collected on roadside trees and in open forests. The variability in thallus color is confusing and it takes some practice to become familiar with all the phases of this lichen.

**58b Upper surface smooth, only faintly pruinose; cortex and me-
dulla K+ yellow (atranorin). Fig. 89.** ....
....*Physcia albicans* (Pers.) Thoms.

Thallus whitish mineral gray, adnate
to closely adnate, 4-6 cm broad; lower
surface dark brown or blackening but
turning whitish along the margins;
apothecia rare. Cortex and medulla
K+ yellow (atranorin). Widespread
at the base of trees in mature forests.
A very close species, *Anaptychia ravenelii* (see p. 49), has a uniformly pale
lower surface and a K+ red medulla.
Anzia ornata (Zahlbr.) Asah., though
quite unrelated, will key out here. It
has dense black tomentum below and
coarsely subisidiate margins. It has been collected several times in
North Carolina and Alabama.

Figure 89.

59a Lobes 1-4 mm wide; thallus adnate to loosely attached. 60

**59b Lobes narrower, 0.3-1.0 mm wide; thallus closely appressed
and usually collected with the substratum.** 67

60a Soredia rather diffuse in irregular soralia. 61

60b Soredia strongly restricted in orbicular soralia. 64

61a Lobes rather broad and irregular, 2-4 mm wide. 62

61b Lobes narrow and linear, 1-3 mm wide. 63

62a Upper cortex continuous; soralia mostly laminal. Fig. 90. ....
....*Parmelia aurulenta* Tuck.

Thallus greenish mineral gray,
adnate, 4-10 cm broad; soredia in
part arising from coarse pustules
(see Fig. 48D) but often quite
powdery; margins very short ciliate, at least in the lobe axils; lower surface densely rhizinate to the
margin; apothecia rare. Cortex
K+ yellow (atranorin); medulla
K+, C+, KC+ yellowish (especially if faint yellow pigment
present). Very common on trees,
more rarely rocks, in forests and

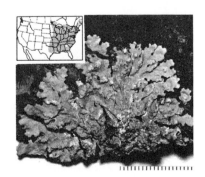

Figure 90.

along roadsides. This is one of the most commonly collected Parmelias, along with *P. caperata* and *P. rudecta*. A very close but rare lichen, *P. crozalsiana* Lesd., may be collected in the central states. It has a wrinkled upper surface, powdery soredia along the ridges, and a K+ yellow medulla (stictic acid).

62b Upper cortex reticulately cracked (with hand lens); soralia toward the margins. ...._Parmelia reticulata_ (see p. 65)

63a Soredia pustulate over the upper surface (with hand lens). Fig. 91. ...._Parmelia formosana_ Zahlbr.

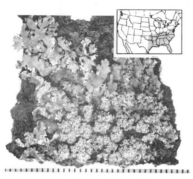

Figure 91.

Thallus whitish mineral gray, closely adnate, 3-8 cm broad; lower surface black, the rhizines dichotomously branched (under lens); apothecia lacking. Cortex orange in UV light (lichexanthone) or UV—; medulla K+ reddish, P+ yellow (unknowns). On pines and deciduous trees in open forest but not commonly collected. In the high mountains of the southern Appalachians one will find *Parmelia croceopustulata* Kurok., which has similar pustules with an orange pigment and a P+ red reaction (protocetraric acid). Superficially the two species are similar.

63b Soredia coarse to pustulate, mostly toward lobe tips. Fig. 92.
...._Parmelia revoluta_ Flk.

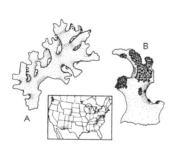

Figure 92. A, thallus (X1); B, soredia (X3).

Thallus mineral gray, adnate, 3-7 cm broad; lobe margins turning under somewhat; lower surface moderately rhizinate, the rhizines branched; apothecia lacking. Cortex K+ yellow (atranorin); medulla C+, KC+ red (gyrophoric acid). Rather rare on large outcrops and on deciduous trees in exposed or open areas, often at higher elevations. *Parmelia sorocheila* Vain. has apical soralia and long marginal cilia with suberect lobes; it will be rarely collected at high elevations in bogs in the southern Appalachians. *P. spumosa* Asah. is C+ red but has mostly laminal pustules, simple rhizines, and short cilia. It is also in the Appalachians.

64a Rhizines dense (under hand lens), forming a narrow mat
around lobe margins. 65
64b Rhizines sparse, not extending beyond the margins. 66
65a Rhizines simple or squarrosely branched (high power lens),
white tipped. (Fig. 94). Fig. 93. ....*Physcia setosa* (Ach.) Nyl.

Thallus mineral gray, adnate, 2-4 cm
broad; rhizines dense; apothecia rare.
Rather rare on maple and other deciduous trees in open forests. This species is
very closely related to *Physcia orbicularis*,
which is about half as large.

Figure 93. (X2).

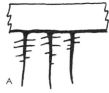

Figure 94.   Types of rhizines. A, squarrosely branched; B,
dichotomously branched.

65b Rhizines dichotomously branched, not white-tipped. (Fig. 94).
Fig. 95. ....*Parmelia rockii* Zahlbr.

Thallus whitish mineral
gray, adnate, 5-12 cm broad;
lower surface black and
densely rhizinate; apothecia
very rare. Cortex K+ yellow
(atranorin); medulla KC+
red (lecanoric and evernic
acids). Common on trunks
of conifers in the Great
Smoky Mountains and moun-
tains of southern Virginia.
Except for the presence of
fumarprotocetraric acid (P+
red, KC−), *P. gondylophora*
Hale is identical and occurs
with *P. rockii. Parmelia lae-
vigata* (Sm.) Ach., which

Figure 95. (X2).

has another chemical reaction (KC+ orange, barbatic acid), occurs rarely in North Carolina and the Black Hills of South Dakota.

66a Soralia conspicuous, strongly capitate. Fig. 96. ....
....*Parmelia cryptochlorophaea* **Hale**

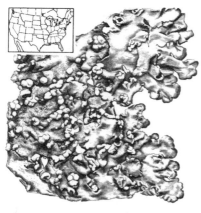

Thallus greenish mineral gray, closely adnate, 5-10 cm broad; upper surface often white-reticulate at the lobe tips; lower surface black and rhizinate but turning brown and naked in a narrow marginal zone; apothecia very rare. Cortex K+ yellow (atranorin); medulla KC+ red (cryptochlorophaeic acid). On deciduous trees along roadsides from Louisiana to Florida.

Figure 96.

66b Soralia smaller, inconspicuous, not strongly capitate. Fig. 97.
....*Parmelia texana* **Tuck.**

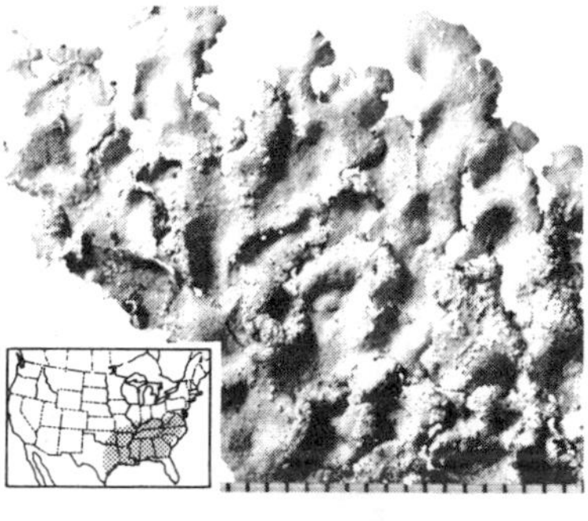

Thallus whitish mineral gray, adnate, 6-12 cm broad; upper surface becoming faintly white-reticulate at the tips; lower surface sparsely rhizinate with a narrow bare zone along the margins; apothecia very rare. Cortex K+ yellow (atranorin); medulla KC+ faint purple (divaricatic acid). Rather rare on conifers and hardwoods in dry open woods or on roadsides. A smaller saxicolous species of similar appearance, *P. alabamensis* Hale & McCull., reacts P+ red (protocetraric acid) and is known only near Birmingham, Alabama, and north into Tennessee. It has narrow linear lobes and occurs on large sandstone cliffs, often with *Dirinaria frostii.*

Figure 97.

67a Thallus mineral to brownish or dark greenish gray, turning green when wet. Fig. 98. ...*Physcia orbicularis* (Neck.) Poetsch.

Thallus closely adnate, 2-6 cm broad; soralia orbicular; medulla white or colored deep reddish orange (K+ purple); lower surface densely rhizinate; apothecia not common. Very common and widespread on deciduous trees everywhere and also on rocks. A form of this lichen, f. *albociliata*, has fine hairs on the upper surface, as in *Physcia ciliata*. The form with a red medulla, f. *rubropulchra*, is often attacked by snails and slugs, leaving the colored medulla exposed.

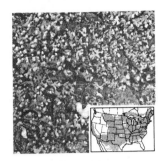

Figure 98.

67b Thallus whitish gray, not turning noticeably green when wet.
....68

68a Lobes discrete and separable, rhizinate below. ....
....*Parmeliopsis hyperopta* (see p. 49)

68b Lobes crowded and more or less fused, closely appressed to subcrustose, rhizines lacking. 69

69a Collected on tree bark. Fig. 99. ....
....*Dirinaria picta* (Sw.) Clem & Schear.

Thallus whitish mineral gray, appressed, 3-5 cm broad, colonies often fusing; soralia becoming dense; apothecia rare. Cortex K+ yellow (atranorin); divaricatic or sekikaic acid in the medulla. Common on deciduous trees in open woods, citrus groves, and along roadsides. *Dirinaria aspera* (Magn.) Awas., a less common lichen, is separated by the coarse pustular or subisidiate scattered soralia. *Physcia tribacoides* has a larger adnate thallus with a pale lower surface.

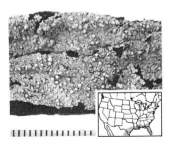

Figure 99.

69b Collected on rocks. 70

70a Collected in temperate eastern North America. Fig. 100. ....
....*Dirinaria frostii* (**Tuck.**) **Awas.**

Thallus whitish mineral gray, tightly appressed, 2-3 cm broad; apothecia rare. Cortex K+ yellow (atranorin). On large outcrops in open woods, often on overhanging ledges. This rarely collected lichen prefers large flat rock surfaces and is usually very difficult to collect.

Figure 100.

70b Collected in western and arctic North America. Fig. 101. ......
....*Placopsis gelida* (**L.**) **Linds.**

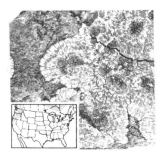

Thallus greenish mineral gray, appressed, chinky-crustose in the center and lobate at the margins, 2-4 cm broad; surface with large tan colored warts (cephalodia), 1-3 mm wide; soralia becoming worn away, leaving pits; apothecia common. Medulla C+, KC+ red (gyrophoric acid). Common on rocks in open areas. This is a pioneer lichen often seen on moist rocks near rivers or moraines.

Figure 101.

71a Lower surface uniformly tan or brown or mottled brown and white (without lens). 72

71b Lower surface black (turning brown along the margins in most species, white in *Parmelia hypotropa*). 77

72a Upper surface wrinkled and ridged (without lens). 73

72b Upper surface not ridged (wrinkled only in older parts). 74

73a **Lower surface mottled brown and white, felty. Fig. 102. Lung-
wort.** ....*Lobaria pulmonaria* **(L.) Hoffm.**

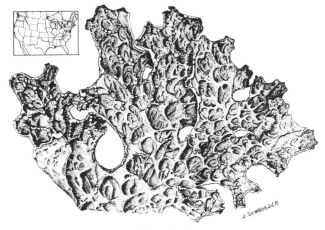

Figure 102.

Thallus light brownish green, turning bright green when wet,
loosely adnate, 5-25 cm broad; soredia often becoming coarsely
isidiate (under lens); apothecia not common. Medulla K+ yellow,
P+ pale orange (stictic and norstictic acids). Widespread in mature northern hardwood forests and swamps but becoming rare in
reforested areas. Sparsely sorediate specimens in the West can be
separated from *Lobaria linita* by the positive K test. This is the
lichen which was widely used in the Middle Ages for treating lung
diseases because of its resemblance to lung tissue.

73b. **Lower surface bare and shiny, felt lacking.** ....
....*Platismatia glauca* **(see p. 70)**

74a **Margins of lobes with cilia (without lens).** ....
....*Parmelia hypotropa* **(see p. 65)**

74b **Margins of lobes without cilia.** **75**

75a Upper cortex with white pores (under low power lens); medulla C+ deep red. Fig. 103. ....*Parmelia subrudecta* Nyl.

Figure 103.

Thallus greenish mineral gray, adnate to loosely attached, 5-10 cm broad; soralia variable, laminal and/or marginal; lower surface pale brown, rhizinate nearly to the margin (see Fig. 6B); apothecia very rare. Cortex K+ yellow (atranorin); medulla C+, KC+ red (lecanoric acid). Common on conifers and deciduous trees in open woods or along roadsides. This was formerly called *P. borreri* (Sm.) Turn., actually a rare species known from Ohio and West Virginia with a blackening lower surface and C+ rose test (gyrophoric acid).

75b Upper cortex continuous, pores lacking; medulla C−. 76
76a Lobes suberect; lower surface bare and shiny. ....*Platismatia glauca* (see p. 70)
76b Lobes adnate; lower surface felty, mottled. Fig. 104. ....*Lobaria scrobiculata* (Scop.) DC.

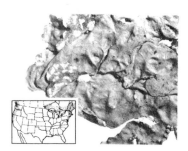

Figure 104.

Thallus light brownish green, loosely adnate, 6-12 cm broad; upper surface and margins sparsely sorediate; apothecia lacking. Medulla K+ yellow, KC+ red, P+ orange (stictic acid and scrobiculin). Rare at the base of trees and on mossy rocks in mature woods. Deforestation in the 19th century probably destroyed most of the habitats for this conspicuous lichen. In the north-

ern Rocky Mountains one may be lucky enough to find *L. hallii*
(Tuck.) Zahlbr., which is close except for having fine hairs and
tomentum on the upper surface.

77a Margins of lobes with cilia (without lens). 78

77b Margins of lobes without cilia. 84

78a Lower surface with a conspicuous broad white rim and black
or dark brown center (without lens). Fig. 105. ....
....*Parmelia hypotropa* Nyl.

Thallus mineral gray, loosely
attached to suberect, 6-12 cm
broad; apothecia lacking. Cortex
K+ yellow (atranorin); medulla
K+ yellow→red, P+ orange
(norstictic acid). Common on the
lower trunks and branches of
hardwoods and conifers in open
woods. The distinct white rim below and chemistry separate this
lichen from *P. rampoddensis* and
P. stuppea. It is the sorediate
phase of *P. perforata.*

Figure 105.

78b Lower surface tan to dark brown at the margins and black at
the center. 79

79a Upper cortex reticulately cracked more or less to the margin
(Fig. 5A) (high power lens). Fig. 106 ....
....*Parmelia reticulata* Tayl.

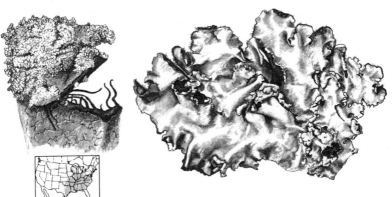

Figure 106.

Thallus light mineral gray, adnate to loosely attached, 6-10 cm broad; soralia variable, powdery to pustulate and coarse, laminal to submarginal; lower surface sparsely rhizinate to the margin; apothecia rare. Cortex K+ yellow (atranorin); medulla K+ yellow→red, P+ orange (salacinic acid). Common in open woods and along roadsides. The reticulate cracking will separate it from *P. stuppea* and *P. margaritata*, both of which intergrade to some extent.

79b Upper cortex continuous (irregularly cracked only on older lobes). 80

80a Soredia laminal, rather diffuse; cilia very short in the lobe axils. ....*Parmelia aurulenta* (see p. 57)

80b Soredia marginal; cilia at lobe tips and in axils. 81

81a Soralia generally linear, the sorediate lobe margins plane (Fig. 107). 82

81b Soralia generally irregular to roundish, submarginal, the sorediate lobe tips rolled under (Fig. 107). 83

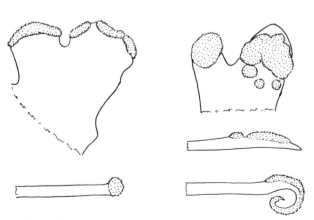

Figure 107. Plane marginal soralia (left) and submarginal and revolute soralia, top and side views.

82a Collected in the Coastal Plain and Piedmont from Virginia to Texas. Fig. 108. ....*Parmelia rampoddensis* **Nyl.**

Thallus whitish mineral gray, loosely attached, 10-30 cm broad; lower surface sparsely rhizinate, naked and brown in a broad marginal zone; apothecia lacking. Cortex K+ yellow (atranorin); medulla KC+ red (alectoronic acid). Common on palm and oak trees in open woods. There is some intergradation with specimens of *P. mellissii* which have exceptionally sorediate isidia.

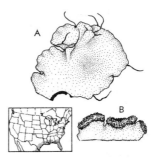

Figure 108. A, thallus (X1); B, marginal soralia (X4).

82b Collected in the Appalachian-Great Lakes region and along the Pacific Coast. Fig. 109. ....*Parmelia stuppea* **Tayl.**

Figure 109.

Thallus mineral gray, loosely adnate, 8-15 cm broad; lower surface with a broad naked marginal zone; apothecia very rare. Cortex K+ yellow (atranorin); medulla K+ yellow→red, P+ orange (salacinic acid). Common on deciduous trees in open woods or swamps, at higher elevations in the Appalachians. *Parmelia margaritata* Hue, a rarer lichen from Iowa and Wisconsin to the Appalachians, has irregular round soralia on short marginal lobes (as in Fig. 107) and a K+ red reaction. It must be carefully distinguished from *P. stuppea*.

83a Medulla K+ yellow. Fig. 110. ...*Parmelia perlata* (Huds.) Ach.

Figure 110. (X1/2).

Thallus mineral gray, loosely adnate, 5-10 cm broad; margins short ciliate; lower surface with a narrow bare zone along the margins; apothecia lacking. Cortex K+ yellow (atranorin); medulla K+ yellow, P+ orange (stictic acid). Quite common on oaks in California but rarer eastward in swamps and open woods. *Parmelia arnoldii* (below) is extremely close and must be distinguished with a color test.

83b Medulla K—. Fig. 111. 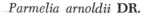...........................*Parmelia arnoldii* DR.

Figure 111.

Thallus light mineral gray, loosely adnate to suberect, 6-12 cm broad; soralia quite small; lobe margins becoming dissected; lower surface with a narrow bare zone along the margin; apothecia lacking. Cortex K+ yellow (atranorin); medulla KC+ red (alectoronic and α-collatolic acid). Rather rare on deciduous trees and cedars in open woods and swamps in the East, more common on conifers in the West. A very rare K— species in Arizona, *P. hababiana* Gyel., has more linear soralia and reacts KC+ red (norlobaridone).

84a Upper cortex with white pores (low power lens). 85

84b Upper cortex continuous, without pores. 86

85a Medulla C+ red; soredia powdery. Fig. 112. ....
.................................*Cetrelia olivetorum* (Nyl.) **Culb. & Culb.**

Thallus greenish mineral gray, loosely attached, 6-20 cm broad; pores 0.1-0.3 mm wide; lower surface with a broad bare zone along the margins; apothecia very rare. Cortex K+ yellow (atranorin); medulla C+, KC+ red (olivetoric acid). Common on trunks and large rock outcrops in open woods. A chemical variant, the rare *C. cetrarioides* (Nyl.) Culb. & Culb., is C— (perlatolic acid). *Cetrelia chicitae* (below) has the same geography but differs in chemistry and soredia. Broad lobed specimens of *Parmelia borreri* (see

Figure 112.

p. 64) and *P. stictica* (see p. 46) may key out here. They have a much narrower bare zone below and different chemistry.

85b Medulla C—; soredia rather coarse and granular. Fig. 113. ....*Cetrelia chicitae* (Culb.) **Culb & Culb.**

Thallus greenish mineral gray, loosely attached, 6-20 cm broad; pores 0.5-1.0 mm wide (visible with naked eye); lower surface with a broad bare marginal zone; apothecia lacking. Cortex K+ yellow (atranorin); medulla KC+ red (alectoronic acid and α-collatolic acid). Common on large rock outcrops, more rarely on trees, in open woods. Closely related *C. olivetorum* has smaller pores and a C+ red reaction.

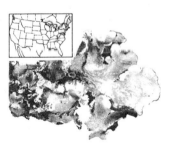

Figure 113.

86a Soredia entirely laminal. 87

86b Soredia marginal. 88

87a Soredia diffuse in broad soralia; some short cilia present in lobe axils. ....*Parmelia aurulenta* (see p. 57)

87b Soredia restricted in small soralia; cilia lacking. ....
....*Parmelia texana* (see p. 60)

88a Thallus suberect; lower surface irregularly mottled white and black or dark brown; collected in boreal and western North America. Fig. 114. ....*Platismatia glauca* (L.) Culb. & Culb.

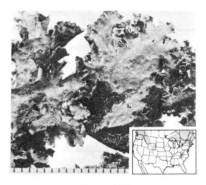

Figure 114.

Thallus greenish mineral gray, loosely attached, 6-15 cm broad; upper surface plane to ridged; soredia rather scattered and in part subisidiate; apothecia lacking. Cortex K+ yellow (atranorin). On conifers in open or exposed areas, quite common in western North America but very rare eastward. This is a most variable species in regard to development of soredia and branching and dissecting of lobes.

88b Thallus not suberect; lower surface not mottled; collected in southeastern United States. 89

89a Medulla K+ yellow→red. Fig. 115. ....*Parmelia cristifera* Tayl.

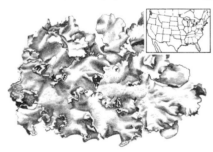

Figure 115.

Thallus whitish mineral gray, loosely adnate, 10-20 cm broad; lower surface with a broad marginal bare zone; apothecia very rare. Cortex K+ yellow (atranorin); medulla K+ red (salacinic acid). Common on oak trees and palms. *Parmelia dilatata* (below) and *P. dominicana* are very close externally but react K− in the medulla.

89b Medulla K− or K+ faint yellow. 90

90a Soralia distinctly crescent-shaped. Fig. 116. ....
....*Parmelia praesorediosa* Nyl.

Figure 116.

Thallus greenish mineral gray, rather closely adnate, 5-10 cm broad; lower surface with a narrow bare zone along the margin; apothecia lacking. Cortex K+ yellow (atranorin); caperatic acid present in the medulla. Common on oak trees in open woods and on citrus trees in groves.

90b Soralia rounded, irregular to linear, not crescent-shaped. 91

91a Lobes 4-15 mm wide, loosely adnate; soralia marginal and irregular or linear. Fig. 117. ....*Parmelia dilatata* **Vain.**
Thallus light mineral gray, adnate to loosely attached, 6-20 cm broad; margins becoming dissected and laciniate, rarely with sparse short cilia; lower surface with a broad bare zone along the margins; apothecia very rare. Cortex K+ yellow (atranorin); medulla P+ red (protocetraric acid). Common on oak trees in open woods and along roadsides. *Parmelia dominicana* Vain., a rarer species, is very close except for the yellowish soralia caused by traces of usnic acid. Rare *P. austrosinensis* Zahlbr. (see Fig. 25) known from Texas to Alabama, has a whitish rim below and reacts P−, C+ red (lecanoric acid).

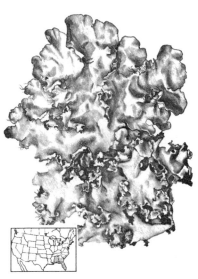

Figure 117.

91b Lobes 3-6 mm wide, adnate; soralia strongly capitate and round. .... *Parmelia cryptochlorophaea* (see p. 60)

ISIDIATE FOLIOSE LICHENS (Fig. 118)

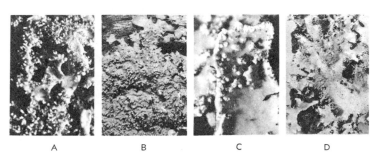

A   B   C   D

Figure 118. Types of isidia. A, B, cylindrical; C, granular; D, flattened.

92a Thallus yellow to yellowish green. 93

92b Thallus not yellow (when dry). 96

93a Lobes broad, 3-10 mm wide, the margins ciliate. 94

93b Lobes narrower, 1-3 mm wide, cilia lacking. 95

94a Medulla sulphur yellow (expose with razor blade). Fig. 119.
....*Parmelia sulphurata* Nees & Flot.

Figure 119.

Thallus yellowish green, adnate, 6-10 cm broad; upper cortex becoming cracked with age, exposing the yellow medulla; lobe margins becoming dissected, isidiate, sparsely ciliate; lower surface with a narrow bare zone along the margins; apothecia lacking. Cortex K+ yellow (atranorin); vulpinic acid in the medulla. Rather rare on hardwoods in mature forests. The most commonly collected *Parmelia* with a yellow medulla will actually be *P. endosulphurea* (p. 83), which has a paler orange medulla and lacks cilia.

94b Medulla white. Fig. 120. ....
................................*Parmelia xanthina* (Müll. Arg.) Vain.

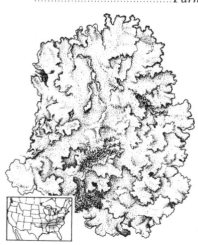

Figure 120.

Thallus yellowish green, loosely adnate, 8-20 cm broad; isidia simple to coralloid; lobe margins becoming dissected and isidiate; lower surface with a broad bare marginal zone; apothecia lacking. Cortex K+ yellow (atranorin); medulla KC— or KC+ red (unknown). On tree trunks and large boulders in open woods. The KC+ red chemical variant is called *P. madagascariacea* (Hue) des Abb.

**95a Lower surface black (sometimes turning brown at the margins).
Fig. 121.** ....*Parmelia conspersa* (Ach.) Ach.

Figure 121.

Thallus yellowish green, adnate (loosely adnate in some specimens from southern United States), 4-12 cm broad, colonies often
fusing to cover very large areas of rock; isidia sparse to dense,
simple; lower surface moderately rhizinate; apothecia common.
Medulla K+ yellow, P+ orange (stictic and norstictic acids). Extremely common on exposed granite and sandstone throughout
North America. Most specimens in eastern North America contain
stictic acid, but there are two other chemical variants that can be
identified only with crystal or color tests: *P. piedmontensis* Hale
(P+ red, K−, fumarprotocetraric acid), rare in the southern Appalachians, and *P. tinctina* Mah. & Gill. (K+ red, salacinic acid), very
rare in the north central states. The brown lower surface will separate otherwise identical *P. plittii* (below).

95b Lower surface uniformly tan to brown. *Parmelia plittii* **Gyel.**
Thallus, chemistry, and distribution as in *P. conspersa* but the
lower surface brown; apothecia common. Very common on exposed
rocks. The chemical variants, which should be identified with crystal tests or chromatography, are *P. mexicana* Gyel. (K+ red, salacinic), very common from southwestern Minnesota south to Texas
and westward to California; *P. subramigera* Gyel. (K−, P+ red,
fumarprotocetraric acid), the most frequently collected variant in
the Piedmont from Virginia to Arkansas; *P. dierythra* Hale (K+
red, norstictic acid alone), rare in South Dakota, Minnesota, and

Wisconsin and *P. kurokawae* Hale (P+ yellow psoromic acid), very rare in western states.

96a Thallus coffee to chestnut brown (dark olive green when wet). **97**

96b Thallus not brown. **102**

97a Isidia thin, cylindrical (Fig. 118A). **98**

97b Isidia in part flattened, papillate, warty, or coarse (Fig. 118 C, D). **99**

98a Lobes 1-3 mm wide; thallus 3-8 cm broad. Fig. 122. ....
....*Parmelia elegantula* **Zahlbr.**

Thallus chestnut brown to olive green, adnate; lower surface brown or blackening, moderately rhizinate; apothecia rare. On trees and rocks in open or exposed areas. This intergrades with *Parmelia exasperatula* (below), which has mostly flattened isidia. Rare *P. chiricahuensis* Anders. & Web. has simple or branched isidia and a K+ red reaction (stictic and norstictic acids); it is known from Arizona. On the whole the western species are poorly known and may be difficult to identify.

Figure 122.

98b Lobes narrow, 0.5-1.0 mm wide; thallus 1-3 cm broad. Fig. 123. ....*Cetraria coralligera* (**W. Web.**) **Hale**

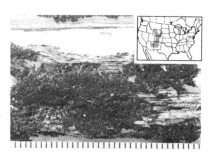

Thallus dark brown, closely adnate; lower surface light brown, sparsely rhizinate; apothecia lacking. Widespread on dead trees and fenceposts. *Cetraria fendleri* has a similar thallus but lacks isidia. The isidiate brown Parmelias are much larger in size.

Figure 123.

99a Isidia in part flattened or lobulate. Fig. 124. ....
....*Parmelia exasperatula* **Nyl.**

Thallus brown to dark olive green, closely adnate, 3-6 cm broad; lower surface black, moderately rhizinate; apothecia lacking. Widespread on conifers and hardwood trees in open woods or along roadsides, rarely also on rocks. *Parmelia elegantula* is close but has cylindrical isidia. *Parmelia panniformis* (Nyl.) Vain., rarely collected on rocks in the north-

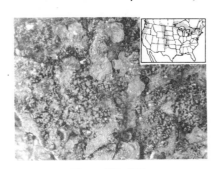

Figure 124. (X3).

ern Rockies, Canada, and upper New York, has very dense flattened isidia that hide the lobes completely.

99b Isidia warty or granular, not flattened. 100

100a Isidia granular to sorediate, easily rubbed off with the fingers, leaving a whitish spot. ....
.........................*Parmelia subaurifera* (see p. 44)

100b Isidia warty to papillate. 101

101a Collected in western North America. ....
.........................*Cetraria platyphylla* (see p. 97)

101b Collected in eastern North America. ....
.........................*Parmelia exasperata* (see p. 101)

102a Lobes narrow, 0.5-4.0 mm wide, often linear. 103

102b Lobes broad, 4-20 mm wide, usually apically rounded. 125

103a Lower surface white, tan, brown, or mottled. 104

103b Lower surface uniformly dark to black (turning brown only in a narrow zone along the margin). 112

104a Tips of lobes with small white pores (use low power lens); isidia thick and flattened. Fig. 125. ......*Parmelia rudecta* Ach.

Figure 125.

Thallus greenish to bluish mineral gray, adnate, 4-12 cm broad; upper surface becoming densely isidiate; lower surface uniformly light tan, densely rhizinate to the margin; apothecia not common. Cortex K+ yellow (atranorin); medulla C+, KC+ red (lecanoric acid). Very common on trees in open woods and along roadsides and on rocks. This is one of the most frequently collected lichens in eastern North America, along with *P. aurulenta* and *P. caperata*.

104b White pores lacking; isidia cylindrical. 105

105a Thallus suberect and appearing subfruticose; lower surface bare. 106

105b Thallus adnate; lower surface with rhizines or tomentum. ...107

106a Isidia laminal; collected in eastern North America and Mexico. ....*Pseudevernia consocians* (see p. 197)

106b Isidia marginal; collected in western North America.
....*Platismatia herrei* (see p. 79)

107a Lower surface white or cream colored (use lens). 108

107b Lower surface tan to dark brown. 109

108a Isidia thin, cylindrical. Fig. 126. ....
....*Parmeliopsis aleurites* (**Ach.**) **Nyl.**

Thallus whitish mineral gray, adnate, 2-5 cm broad; isidia often becoming dense (see Fig. 118A); lower surface sparsely rhizinate; apothecia very rare. Cortex K+ deep yellow (thamnolic acid). Common on bark of conifers and on dead stumps in open woods, rarely on rocks. This species may be confused with *Parmelia dissecta*, which is black below and ciliate.

Figure 126.

108b Isidia barrel-shaped and granular. Fig. 127. ....
....*Anaptychia granulifera* (**Ach.**) **Mass.**

Thallus light mineral gray, adnate, 3-6 cm broad; isidia moderate, constricted at the base; lower surface moderately rhizinate; apothecia rare. Cortex K+ yellow (atranorin); medulla K+ yellow→red, P+ orange (salacinic acid). On deciduous trees in open woods.

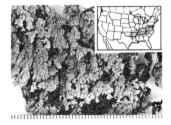

Figure 127.

109a Lobes narrow, 0.5 2.0 mm wide. **110**

109b Lobes broader and irregular, 2-6 mm wide. **111**

110a Margins of lobes with small black inflated cilia (use high power lens). Fig. 128. ....*Parmelia scortella* **Nyl.**
Thallus whitish mineral gray (often turning buff in the herbarium), closely adnate, 3-6 cm broad; upper surface sparsely to moderately isidiate; lower surface brown or darkening; apothecia not common. Cortex K+ yellow (atranorin); medulla C+, KC+ red (gyrophoric acid). Widespread on tree trunks and branches in open woods. Superficially it is very close to *P. laevigatula*, which is black below and contains lecanoric acid.

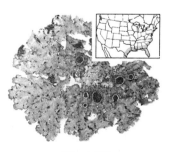

Figure 128.

110b Margins without cilia. Fig. 129. ....
....*Pannaria pityrea* (**DC.**) **Degel.**

Thallus brownish mineral gray to light brown, closely adnate, 4-6 cm broad; isidia mostly marginal, whitish pruinose at the tips; lower surface light brown, densely tomentose; apothecia rare. Medulla P+ red (pannarin) or P–. At the base of trees or on mosses over rocks in mature woods. When very closely adnate it resembles *Pannaria leucosticta*, which lacks distinct lobation. The algae are blue-green, and this character, along with tomentum, will separate it from species of *Parmelia* or *Anaptychia*.

Figure 129.

111a Upper cortex finely cracked (use low power lens); medulla K–. ....*Parmelia caroliniana* (see p. 80)

111b Upper cortex continuous; medulla K+ red. Fig. 130. ....
....*Parmelia salacinifera* **Hale**

Thallus mineral gray, turning buff in the herbarium, adnate, 6-10 cm broad; upper surface moderately to sparsely isidiate; lower surface tan, moderately rhizinate; apothecia lacking. Cortex K+ yellow (atranorin); medulla K+ yellow→red (salacinic acid). On oak and palm trees in Florida. It often occurs with *P. amazonica* (below), which has a black lower surface and K– reaction.

Figure 130. (X2).

112a Medulla pale yellow orange (section with razor blade under lens); collected on rocks (rarely on bark). Fig. 131. ....
....*Parmelia obsessa* **Ach.**

Thallus greenish mineral gray, closely adnate, 3-6 cm broad; upper surface becoming densely isidiate; margins with very short cilia, especially in the axils; lower surface densely rhizinate; apothecia rare. Cortex K+ yellow (atranorin); medulla K+, C+, KC+ yellow, P+ orange (galbinic acid and unknowns). Common on large outcrops in

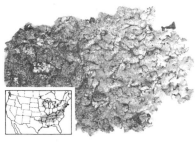

Figure 131.

open woods. This lichen may be difficult to collect because it prefers broad flat surfaces of hard rocks.

112b Medulla white; collected on bark, less commonly on rock.
....**113**

113a Thallus suberect; lower surface bare and shiny; collected in western North America. Fig. 132. ....
....*Platismatia herrei* (Imsh.)Culb. & Culb.

Thallus greenish mineral gray, loosely attached, 4-8 cm broad; lobes often slightly convoluted; isidia round to flattened and branched, concentrated along the margins; lower surface variable, nearly white to brown or black or mottled; apothecia lacking. Cortex K+ yellow (atranorin); fatty acids also present. Common on trunks and branches of exposed conifers. This lichen is much narrower than *Platismatia glauca. P. stenophylla* is very similar except for lacking soredia.

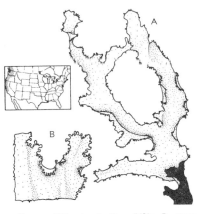

Figure 132. A, thallus (X2); B, marginal soralia (X4).

113b Thallus adnate; lower surface with rhizines or tomentum; collected in eastern North America (only *Parmelia saxatilis* also in western States). **114**

114a Tips of lobes with angular white markings (see Fig. 5B), weakly ridged (use low power lens). Fig. 133. ....
....*Parmelia saxatilis* (L.) Ach.

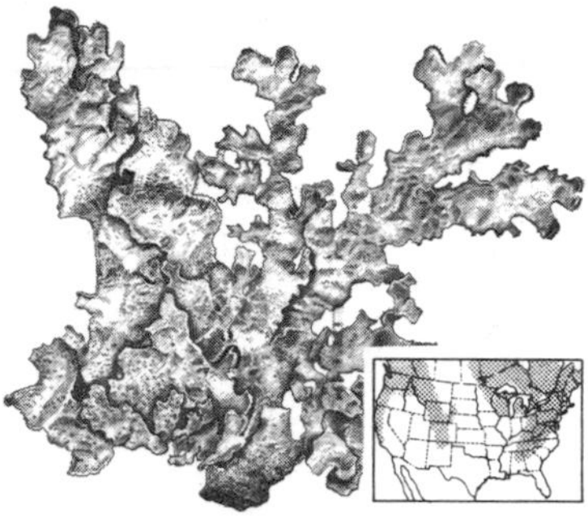

Figure 133.

Thallus whitish to greenish mineral gray, adnate, 4-10 cm broad; isidia coarse to granular (see Fig. 118C), occurring mostly on ridges and the margin; lower surface densely rhizinate, the rhizines simple (western North America) or squarrose (eastern North America); apothecia not common. Cortex K+ yellow (atranorin); medulla K+ yellow →red (salacinic acid with or without lobaric acid). Widespread on trees and boulders in open woods or along roadsides. A frequent companion species is *Parmelia sulcata*, which has soredia. *P. pseudosulcata* Gyel. from Oregon and Washington is identical except for chemistry (K—, protocetraric acid).

114b Tips of lobes without distinct white markings, not ridged.
....115

115a Lobes short and irregular, 2-6 mm wide. 116

115b Lobes narrow and linear, 0.5-3.0 mm wide. 119

116a Lobe margins short ciliate (use low power lens). ....
.... *Parmelia crinita* (see p. 84)

116b Lobes without cilia. 117

117a Upper surface finely cracked (under lens). Fig. 134.
....*Parmelia caroliniana* Nyl.

Thallus greenish mineral gray, adnate, 5-10 cm broad; upper surface moderately isidiate; lower surface black or dark brown, naked in a narrow marginal zone; apothecia rare. Cortex K+ yellow (atranorin); medulla KC+ faint purple (perlatolic acid). Common in open woods, often on conifers, more rarely on rocks. It resembles *Parmelia rudecta* which differs in being C+ red and in having a very pale lower surface.

Figure 134.

117b Upper surface continuous. 118

118a Lower surface densely tomentose; thallus slate or dark mineral gray. Fig. 135. ....*Coccocarpia cronia* (Tuck.) Vain.

Thallus adnate, 1-4 cm broad; isidia moderate, simple; lower surface variable, gray to blackening, tomentum matted; apothecia very rare. Widespread at the base of deciduous trees and on shaded rocks in mature woods. The nonisidiate relative is *Coccocarpia parmelioides.*

Figure 135.

118b Lower surface sparsely rhizinate (use lens); thallus whitish mineral gray. ....*Parmelia amazonica* Nyl.

Thallus superficially as in *Parmelia salacinifera* but with a black lower surface; apothecia lacking. Cortex K+ yellow (atranorin); medulla P+ red (protocetraric acid). On oaks and palm trees in Florida, often occurring with *P. salacinifera.*

119a Lobe margins short ciliate or bulbate ciliate (under high power lens). 120

119b Lobe margins smooth, without cilia (but sometimes with short rhizines projecting from below). 123

120a Cilia simple, not inflated (high power lens). 121

120b Cilia inflated at the base. 122

121a Isidia cylindrical; medulla C+ red. Fig. 136. ....
....*Parmelia dissecta* Nyl.

Thallus light mineral gray, adnate, 3-7 cm broad; upper surface moderately isidiate; lower surface moderately rhizinate, the rhizines simple; apothecia rare. Cortex K+ yellow (atranorin); medulla C+, KC+ red (gyrophoric acid). Common on exposed trees or rocks in dry areas. *Parmelia horrescens* (below)

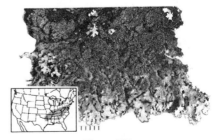

Figure 136.

often occurs with this species and must be carefully distinguished from it with the C test. Specimens with a yellow medulla are probably *P. obsessa* (see p. 78).

121b Isidia partly cylindrical, partly flattened, often tipped with short cilia; medulla C—. Fig. 137. ....*Parmelia horrescens* Tayl.

Figure 137. (X15).

Thallus light mineral gray, adnate, 2-4 cm broad; isidia moderate to dense; lower surface sparsely to moderately rhizinate; apothecia rare. Cortex K+ yellow (atranorin). Fairly widespread over the same range as *Parmelia dissecta*, occurring on deciduous trees or conifers.

122a Lower surface black; medulla C+ deep red. Fig. 138. ....
....*Parmelia laevigatula* **Nyl.**

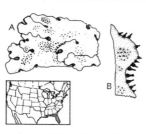

Figure 138. A, thallus (X3;) B, bulbate cilia (X20).

Thallus whitish mineral gray, closely adnate, 3-8 cm broad; isidia short, sparse to quite dense; lower surface densely rhizinate, the rhizines black, branched; apothecia common. Cortex K+ yellow (atranorin); medulla C+, KC+ red (lecanoric acid). On branches and trunks of deciduous trees in open woods. This unusual species is closely related to *P. scortella* but has a black lower surface.

122b Lower surface dark brown to blackening at the center; medulla C+ rose. ....*Parmelia scortella* Nyl. (see p. 77)
123a Isidia all thin and cylindrical. 124
123b Isidia in part flattened and lobulate (Fig. 118D). Fig. 139.
....*Parmelia prolongata* **Kurok.**

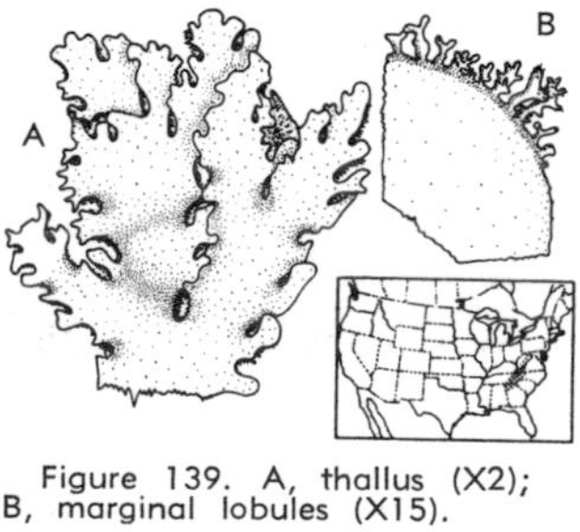

Figure 139. A, thallus (X2); B, marginal lobules (X15).

Thallus light mineral gray, adnate, 5-10 cm broad; lower surface densely rhizinate, the rhizines dichotomously branched; apothecia lacking. Cortex K+ yellow (atranorin); medulla C+, KC+ red (anziaic acid). On bark of spruce and fir at high elevations in the Great Smoky Mountains in North Carolina and in southern Virginia. This often occurs with *Parmelia rockii* but is not as common. An associated species, *P. ensifolia* Kurok., is very close but is C–, KC+ red (alectoronic acid).

**124a Rhizines conspicuous, dichotomously branched (under lens).
Fig. 140.** .... *Parmelia imbricatula* Zahlbr.
Thallus light mineral gray, adnate, 5-10 cm broad; upper surface sparsely to moderately isidiate; apothecia very rare. Cortex K+ yellow (atranorin); medulla C+, KC+ orange (barbatic acid and unknowns). Rare on deciduous trees in western North Carolina. *Parmelia dentella* Hale & Kurok., known from Cheaha Park, Alabama, and Buncombe Co., North Carolina, is very similar but occurs on rocks and is P+ orange (echinocarpic acid), C–, KC–.

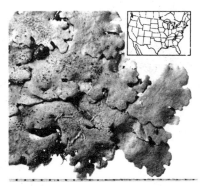

Figure 140.

124b Rhizines sparse, simple. .... *Parmelia dissecta* (see p. 81)

125a Medulla yellow orange (section with razor blade). ....
....*Parmelia endosulphurea* (Hillm.) Hale

Thallus externally the same as *Parmelia tinctorum* (see p. 87); apothecia very rare. Cortex K+ yellow (atranorin); medulla C+, KC+ deeper yellow (unknowns). On oak trees in open woods from Texas to Florida. It has been confused with *P. sulphurata* (see p. 72) which has a yellowish thallus and deep sulphur yellow medulla. Except for the pigmented medulla, it is very close to *P. tinctorum*.

125b Medulla all white. 126

126a Lobe margins with black cilia (low power lens). 127

126b Lobe margins smooth, without cilia. ....,,...........131

127a Lower surface brown or dark brown. Fig. 141. ....
....*Parmelia subtinctoria* **Zahlbr.**

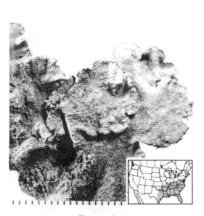

Figure 141.

Thallus greenish mineral gray (sometimes turning buff in the herbarium), loosely adnate, 5-10 cm broad; upper surface densely isidiate, the cortex shiny and faintly white-spotted; lower surface rhizinate or papillate nearly to the margin; apothecia lacking. Cortex K+ yellow (atranorin); medulla K— or K+ yellow→red, KC+ red (norlobaridon with or without salacinic acid). Fairly common on deciduous trees in open woods or along roadsides. The K— population without salacinic acid is a chemical strain called *P. haitiensis* Hale. The species intergrades morphologically with *P. crinita* and *P. subcrinita*, both of which have a black lower side with a broad bare zone along the margins.

127b Lower surface black (with a dark brown zone at the margin). 128

128a Medulla K—; isidia mostly marginal, becoming sorediate. Fig. 142. ....*Parmelia mellissii* **Dodge**

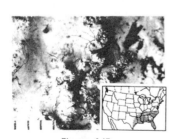

Figure 142.

Thallus whitish mineral gray, loosely adnate, 5-10 cm broad; isidia variable in density and development of soredia; lower surface sparsely rhizinate; apothecia lacking. Cortex K+ yellow (atranorin); medulla KC+ red (alectoronic acid). Widespread in open woods but not often collected. *Parmelia crinita* is similar in external appearance but reacts K+ yellow in the medulla.

128b Medulla K+ yellow or yellow turning red. 129

129a Medulla K+ persistently yellow; isidia becoming dense, often with apical cilia. Fig. 143. ....*Parmelia crinita* **Ach.**

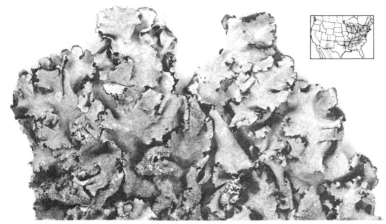

Figure 143.

Thallus whitish to greenish mineral gray, loosely adnate, 6-12 cm broad; isidia becoming branched and coralloid; lower surface with a narrow bare zone at the margin; apothecia rare. Cortex K+ yellow (atranorin); medulla K+ yellow (stictic acid). Common on trunks of oaks, maples, and other hardwoods as well as cedar in open woods and on rocks. *Parmelia internexa* Nyl., a poorly known species from southeastern United States, is separated primarily by narrow lobes, 2-4 mm wide. *P. subcrinita* generally has sparser isidia, broader lobes, and reacts K+ red in the medulla.

129b Medulla K+ yellow turning deep red after a minute; isidia sparser, not tipped with cilia. 130

130a Upper surface continuous (cracked in older parts); lower surface with a broad bare zone at the margin, 3-4 mm wide. Fig. 144. ....*Parmelia subcrinita* Nyl.

Thallus whitish mineral gray, loosely adnate, 5-15 cm broad; upper surface becoming whitish pruinose with age; lower surface sparsely rhizinate; apothecia lacking. Cortex K+ yellow (atranorin); medulla K+ yellow→red, P+ orange (salacinic acid). Common on deciduous trees and rocks in open woods.

Figure 144.

130b Upper surface reticulately cracked to the margin (use low power lens); lower surface with a narrow bare or papillate zone. Fig. 145. ....*Parmelia subisidiosa* (Müll. Arg.) **Dodge**

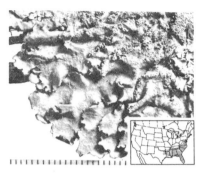

Figure 145.

Thallus light mineral gray, adnate, 4-10 cm broad; isidia rather irregular, becoming granular, often near the lobe margins; apothecia lacking. Cortex K+ yellow (atranorin); medulla K+ yellow →red, P+ orange (salacinic acid). Rare on trees in open woods. It is very closely related to *Parmelia reticulata*, which is sorediate and has the same type of cracking. There is some intergradation with *P. subcrinita* (above).

131a Upper surface ridged and wrinkled (without lens). Fig. 146. ....*Platismatia norvegica* (Lynge) **Culb. & Culb.**

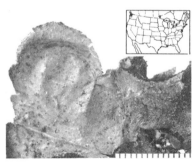

Figure 146.

Thallus light mineral gray, loosely adnate to suberect, 8-12 cm broad; lower surface wrinkled, bare to sparsely rhizinate; apothecia lacking. Cortex K+ yellow (atranorin); fatty acids also present. Rare on branches of conifers. Though very close to *Platismatia lacunosa* and *P. tuckermanii*, this species is easily separated by the isidia.

131b Upper surface plane to slightly wrinkled but not ridged. 132

132a Upper cortex with small white pores (use hand lens); isidia in part flattened. .... *Parmelia rudecta* (see p. 76)

132b Upper cortex without pores (but with some faint white markings at lobe tips in *Parmelia caroliniana*). 133

133a Lobes broad and rounded at the tips, 5-15 mm wide; medulla C+ deep red. Fig. 147. ....*Parmelia tinctorum* **Nyl.**

Figure 147.

Thallus whitish mineral gray, adnate to loosely attached, 8-20 cm broad; isidia sparse to moderate, sometimes rather granular; lower surface with a broad bare brown zone (see Fig. 3); apothecia rare. Cortex K+ yellow (atranorin); medulla C+, KC+ (lecanoric acid). Very common on trees and rocks in open woods and along roadsides. This is one of the most frequently collected lichens in the southern United States. Larger forms of *P. amazonica* that key here can be recognized by the C—, P+ red reaction.

133b Lobes much narrower, 3-6 mm wide; medulla C—. 134

134a Medulla K+ yellow→red. ...*Parmelia salacinifera* (see p. 78)

134b Medulla K—. 135

135a Dense tomentum on the lower surface; thallus slate-gray. .... *Coccocarpia cronia* (see p. 81)

135b Sparse rhizines on the lower surface; thallus whitish mineral gray. ....*Parmelia caroliniana* (see p. 80)

FOLIOSE LICHENS WITHOUT SOREDIA OR ISIDIA

136a Thallus orange, the upper surface and apothecia K+ purple. 137

136b Thallus not orange (medulla may be orange in some Physcias and *Solorina crocea*). 138

137a Collected on rocks. Fig. 148. ....

....*Caloplaca elegans* (**Link**) **Th. Fr.**

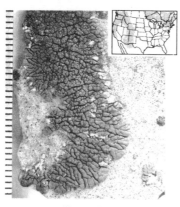

Figure 148.

Thallus closely adnate to appressed, 2-5 cm broad; lower surface white, rhizines lacking; apothecia very common. Cortex K+ purple (parietin). Common on exposed cliffs and boulders throughout western North America but rarer eastward. This is an extremely variable lichen in terms of adnation and crowding of lobes. Subcrustose specimens with appressed parallel lobes are called *C. murorum* (Hoffm.) Th. Fr. On rocks near the shore in Maine and Nova Scotia one will also find *C. scopularis* (Nyl.) Lett., which has very narrow lobes (about 0.25 mm wide). Distinct raised lobes are characteristic of *C. trachyphylla* (Tuck.) Zahlbr., which intergrades with *C. elegans* in western North America.

137b Collected on trees. Fig. 149. ....

....*Xanthoria polycarpa* (**Ehrh.**) **Oliv.**

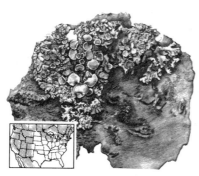

Figure 149.

Thallus closely adnate, 1-3 cm broad; lobes often crowded and hidden by the numerous apothecia; lower surface white, sparsely rhizinate. Cortex K+ purple (parietin). Common on twigs, branches, and trunks of exposed trees. This species is commonly collected on aspen trees. A much larger spreading lichen, *X. parietina* (L.) Th. Fr., will be found on trees and rocks along the Atlantic Coast from Massachusetts northward.

138a Thallus yellow to yellow green (when dry). 139

138b Thallus not yellow. 156

139a Thallus crustose and chinky at the center, minutely lobed at the margins. 140

140a Disk of apothecia black; spores brown, two-celled (use microscope). Fig. 150. .... *Rinodina oreina* (Ach.) Mass.

Thallus greenish yellow, closely appressed, 2-6 cm broad; lower surface dark, without rhizines; apothecia very common. Medulla C+, KC+ red (gyrophoric acid), or C−; P− or P+ red (fumarprotocetraric acid). Widespread on hard acidic granites and quartzite in open exposed areas throughout North America.

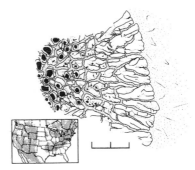

Figure 150.

140b Disk brown; spores colorless, one-celled. Fig. 151. ....
....*Lecanora muralis* (Schreb.) Ach.

Thallus dull greenish yellow, 2-6 cm broad; lower surface white, rhizines lacking; lobe margins often black rimmed; apothecia very common. Medulla P− or P+ red (fumarprotocetraric acid). Widespread on sandstone, granites, and calcareous rocks in open areas. This species is commonly found in stone walls and on stone steps in farm yards. The commonest member of this group in the western states is *Lecanora novomexicana* Magn., a larger more robust plant without a black margin. It is abundant in semiarid regions, and from a distance it looks like a yellow *Parmelia*.

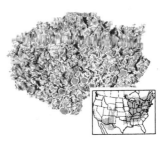

Figure 151.

142a On soil in arctic or alpine areas. Fig. 152. ....
....Nephroma arcticum (L.) Torss.

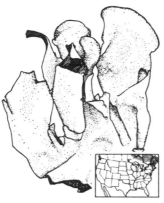

Thallus yellowish green, loosely attached on soil and among mosses, 6-15 cm broad; lower surface black and short tomentose at the center, tan toward the margin; apothecia common, up to 2 cm in diameter, on the lower surface of lobe tips. Widespread and conspicuous. This is one of the most unusual arctic lichens.

Figure 152.

142b On trees in temperate or boreal localities. 143

143a Upper surface ridged (without lens); lobe margins lobulate. Fig. 153. ....Lobaria oregana (Tuck.) Müll. Arg.

Thallus light greenish yellow, loosely attached, 10-25 cm broad; lower surface mottled brown and cream, short tomentose; apothecia rare. Medulla K+ yellow, P+ orange (stictic acid). Common on conifers in open woods or on mossy rocks. The ridged upper surface is similar to that of *Lobaria linita* and *L. pulmonaria* but the color and chemistry differ. A rare western lichen, *Cetraria pallidula* Tuck., will key here; it is smaller (up to 8 cm broad) and has marginal apothecia and pycnidia.

Figure 153.

143b Upper surface not ridged; lobules lacking. Fig. 154. ....
....*Parmelia praesignis* **Nyl.**

Thallus greenish yellow, adnate, 6-15 cm broad; upper surface with white pores (pseudocyphellae); lower surface black and sparsely rhizinate; apothecia common. Medulla C+, KC+ red (lecanoric acid). Common on tree trunks in open woods. This conspicuous lichen is the nonsorediate form of the common *P. flaventior* (see p. 41). In southern Arizona one may collect *P. darrovii* Thoms., a rare variant with a uniformly tan lower surface.

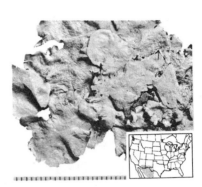

Figure 154.

144a Collected on rocks or soil. 145

144b Collected on tree bark. 150

145a Lower surface uniformly white, tan, or brown. 146

145b Lower surface black (dark brown only at the margin). 149

146a Collected on rocks. 147

146b Collected on soil in the prairies. Fig. 155. ....
.... *Parmelia chlorochroa* **Tuck.**

Thallus greenish yellow, leathery, composed of separate groups of scattered lobes, the margins turning under, 2-3 cm long; lower surface tan to brown, sparsely rhizinate; apothecia very rare. Medulla K+ yellow→red, P+ orange (salacinic acid or rarely stictic acid). Locally abundant growing loose on soil among prairie grasses. This distinctive lichen intergrades with western forms of *P. taractica* (see p. 92), which has more flattened lobes and a coherent thallus. Another free growing soil lichen is *Lecanora haydenii* Tuck., which lacks rhizines, is K−, and occurs in Wyoming, South Dakota, and western Nebraska.

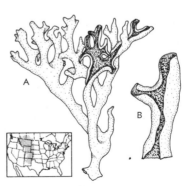

Figure 155. A, thallus (X2); B, lobe tip (X5).

147a Lower surface tan or brown. 148

147b Lower surface white. Fig. 156. ....
....Parmelia centrifuga (L.) Ach.

Figure 156.

• Thallus pale greenish yellow, closely adnate, often forming concentric bands, 3-10 cm broad; lower surface sparsely rhizinate; apothecia rare. Medulla KC+ red (alectoronic acid). Common on rocks in arctic regions, rarer southward along the northern Great Lakes shore line and high elevations in the Appalachians. A related species known only from tundra regions is *Parmelia separata* Th. Fr., which has a black lower surface.

148a Thallus quite closely attached and not easily removed except with a knife. Fig. 157. ....*Parmelia cumberlandia* (Gyel.) Hale

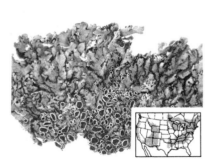

Figure 157.

Thallus greenish yellow, adnate, 3-12 cm broad; lower surface tan to brown, moderately rhizinate; apothecia common. Medulla K+ yellow, P+ orange (stictic and norstictic acids). Widespread and common on exposed rocks. A K+ red (salacinic acid) variant is called *Parmelia lineola* Berry; it occurs widely in the western states. Another western species, *P. arseneana* Gyel., contains stictic acid but is very closely appressed to subcrustose. Two rare variants also occur in the West: *P. novomexicana* Gyel. (P+ red, fumarprotocetraric acid) and *P. psoromifera* Kurok. (P+ yellow, psoromic acid). Chemical tests must be made on all of these.

148b Thallus loosely attached and easily removed from the rock by hand. Fig. 158. ....*Parmelia taractica* Kremplh.

Thallus greenish yellow, 4-15 cm broad; lobes quite elongate and linear; lower surface tan, moderately rhizinate; apothecia common. Medulla K+ yellow→red, P+ orange (salacinic acid). Widespread on exposed acidic rocks but not as common as *P. cumberlandia.* This is a variable species that intergrades with both *P. chlorochroa,* which is free on soil, and with *P. lineola,* which is more adnate. Specimens with a black lower surface are *P. tasmanica* (see below).

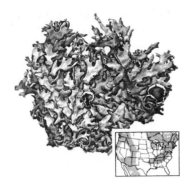

Figure 158.

149a Thallus closely adnate on rock and difficult to remove without a knife ....*Parmelia hypopsila* **Müll. Arg.**

Thallus, chemistry, and distribution as in *Parmelia cumberlandia* (see above) but the lower surface black, turning brown only at the margins. This lichen is considerably rarer than *P. cumberlandia.* A chemical variant with fumarprotocetraric acid (K−, P+ red) is called *P. hypomelaena* Hale; it occurs rather frequently in Arkansas and adjacent states.

149b Thallus loosely attached and easily removed by hand or with a knife. ....*Parmelia tasmanica* **Hook. & Tayl.**

Thallus, chemistry, and distribution as in *P. taractica* but the lower surface black, turning brown only at the margins. This species appears to be quite common and often occurs with *P. taractica.*

150a Lobes finely divided, 0.3-0.5 mm wide. Fig. 159. ....
............................*Candelaria fibrosa* **(Fr.) Müll. Arg.**

Thallus greenish lemon yellow, 1-2 cm broad, closely adnate; lower surface white, sparsely rhizinate; apothecia numerous, with rhizines around the base. Cortex K+ yellowish (calycin). Widespread on deciduous trees in open woods or along roadsides. This is the nonsorediate counterpart of *Candelaria concolor* (see p. 42), which is much more common.

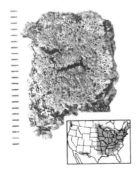

Figure 159.

150b Lobes broader, 1-3 mm wide, not finely divided. 151

151a Medulla deep sulphur yellow (exposed with razor blade). Fig. 160. ....*Cetraria viridis* Schwein.

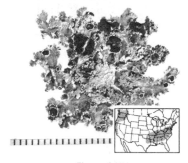

Figure 160.

Thallus light yellowish green, adnate, 2-3 cm broad; lower surface light yellow, sparsely rhizinate; apothecia common. Vulpinic acid in the medulla. Widespread but rather rare on branches of deciduous trees in open woods. This species often grows in the canopies of trees. In the western States one will collect *C. canadensis* Räs., a larger and deeper yellow species that has been called *C. juniperina.*

151b Medulla white or very pale yellow orange. 152

152a Collected from Saskatchewan and Montana westward. Fig. 161. ....*Parmelia sphaerosporella* Müll. Arg.

Figure 161.

Thallus light yellowish green, closely adnate, 4-8 cm broad; upper surface finely wrinkled (without lens); lower surface buff to white, moderately rhizinate; apothecia common. Widespread on conifers in open woods. The pale lower surface distinguishes this unusual lichen from *Parmelia caperata* and other yellow Parmelias.

152b Collected in eastern and southern North America. 153

153a Collected on scrub pine trees. Fig. 162. ....
....*Cetraria aurescens* Tuck.

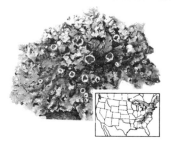

Figure 162.

Thallus light yellowish green, adnate, 2-6 cm broad; upper surface somewhat ridged (without lens); lower surface light tan, sparsely rhizinate; apothecia and pycnidia common. Common on trunks and branches of pine trees in open woodlots. It is often collected with *Parmeliopsis placorodia.*

153b Collected on deciduous or hardwoods trees or on cypress.
....154

**154a Lower surface black (brown only at the very margin). Fig.
163.** ....*Parmelia rutidota* **Hook. & Tayl.**

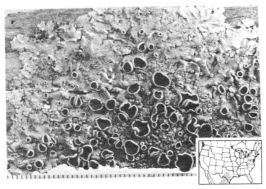

Figure 163.

Thallus yellowish green, closely adnate, 4-8 cm broad; lower surface moderately rhizinate with a narrow bare zone at the margin; apothecia common. Medulla P+ red (protocetraric acid). Common on trees in open areas. This species is very close to *P. caperata* except for the lack of soredia.

154b Lower surface tan or brown. 155

**155a Collected in the Coastal Plain from North Carolina to Texas.
Fig. 164.** ....*Parmelia congruens* **Ach.**

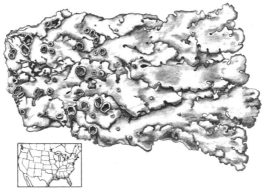

Figure 164. (X2).

Thallus pale yellowish mineral gray, closely adnate, 5-10 cm broad; medulla white to pale yellow orange; lower surface pale buff; moderately rhizinate; apothecia very common. Medulla K+, C+, KC+ deeper yellow (unknowns). Common on shaded lower trunks of deciduous trees and cypress in mature woods.

155b **Collected in the Appalachian-Great Lakes region.** ....
.... *Parmelia cumberlandia* (see p. 92)

156a **Thallus brown, varying from blackish to olive brown.** 157

156b **Thallus not brown.** 172

157a **Thallus about 1 cm broad, the lobes crowded, often covered with apothecia.** 158

157b **Thallus 2-10 cm broad, the apothecia (if present) not crowded.**
....159

158a **Apothecia crowded and heaped; thallus not changing color when wet. Fig. 165.** ....*Cetraria sepincola* (Ehrh.) **Ach.**

Figure 165.

Thallus dark brown, adnate but sometimes easily plucked from twigs, round, about 1 cm broad; margins of lobes rarely ciliate; lower surface tan, sparsely rhizinate; apothecia. numerous. Common on twigs of alder, birch, and other deciduous trees and conifers, often in open bogs or swamps. Though much smaller than *Cetraria ciliaris*, these two species are very close and sometimes intergrade. Another similar species collected in the western States can be identified as *C. merrillii* DR., a somewhat larger lichen with a ridged surface and incised margins.

158b **Apothecia separate to touching, not crowded together; thallus turning green when wet. Fig. 166.** ....
....*Cetraria fendleri* (Nyl.) **Tuck.**

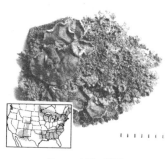

Figure 166. (X4).

Thallus dark greenish olive to brown, very closely adnate, 0.5-2.0 cm broad; lower surface tan, sparsely rhizinate; apothecia numerous. Common on branches and trunks of scrub pines and other conifers in open woods or along roadsides. This should not be confused with juvenile specimens of *Cetraria ciliaris*, which has much broader lobes (at least 1 mm wide). It is frequently overlooked because the thallus color blends with the conifer bark.

159a Thallus suberect and loosely attached; lobe margins with tiny black pycnidia (use lens) and apothecia. 160

159b Thallus more or less uniformly adnate; apothecia and pycnidia (if present) laminal (apical on lower surface in *Nephroma*). 161

160a Lobes 1-3 mm wide, smooth. Fig. 167. ....*Cetraria ciliaris* Ach.

Thallus light greenish brown to olive or dark brown, 3-7 cm broad; upper surface weakly wrinkled (use lens); margins smooth or very short ciliate; lower surface white to tan, very sparsely rhizinate; apothecia numerous. Medulla C— or C+ red (olivetoric acid), KC— or KC+ red (alectoronic acid). Very common on conifers, deciduous trees, and fenceposts in open woods or along roadsides. Plants with alectoronic acid may be classified as *Cetraria halei* Culb., by far the most common chemical variant

Figure 167.

in the Great Lakes region; those with a C—, KC— reaction as *C. orbata* (Tuck.) Nyl., rather rare in the East but more common on the West Coast; and those C+ red as the typical strain, *C. ciliaris*, which is especially common in southeastern United States.

160b Lobes broader, 4-8 cm broad, becoming warty (without lens). Fig. 168. ....*Cetraria platyphylla* Tuck.

Thallus chestnut brown, 3-8 cm broad; upper surface and rim of apothecia rugose, warty or subpapillate to coarsely isidiate; lobe margins becoming dissected; lower surface wrinkled, light brown, sparsely rhizinate; apothecia common. Widespread on exposed conifers. Superficially it resembles robust specimens of *Cetraria ciliaris* or *C. merrillii*, both of which lack warts.

Figure 168.

161a Lobe margins and surface with small squamules (with lower power lens). Fig. 169. ......*Nephroma helveticum* (Ach.) Ach.

Figure 169. (X2).

Thallus light brown, loosely adnate, 4-8 cm broad; lower surface light brown to blackening with a thin felty layer (tomentum); apothecia common, located on the lower surface at the tips. Widespread at the base of trees and on mossy rocks in woodlots or along roadsides. This is the most commonly collected *Nephroma* in the United States. Though completely unrelated, brownish specimens of *Anaptychia palmatula* (see p. 105) will key out here; it has much narrower lobes (1-2 mm) and rhizines below as well as numerous laminal apothecia.

161b Squamules lacking or only sparsely developed. 162
162a Apothecia present on lower surface of lobe tips. Fig. 170.
....*Nephroma bellum* (Spreng.) Tuck.

Figure 170.

Thallus light brown, loosely attached to adnate, 4-8 cm broad; lower surface tan or darkening, smooth and bare; apothecia common. Medulla K— or K+ faint yellow (unknowns). At the base of trees or on rocks in open woods or along roadsides. A very close relative, *N. laevigatum* Ach. has a similar range but the medulla is distinctly pale yellow and K+ deep yellow. Specimens with a thin layer of tomentum below are *N. resupinatum* (L.) Ach., a rarer species along the west coast and eastward in the boreal forests.

162b Apothecia (if present) on the surface of the lobes. 163

163a Collected on rocks. 164

163b Collected on tree bark. 166

164a Collected on rocks near or submerged in streams; lobes crowded, turning green when wet. Fig. 171. ....
...............................*Dermatocarpon fluviatile* (G. Web.) Th. Fr.

Thallus light brown, adnate to loosely attached, 1-4 cm broad; lobes irregular, often crowded; upper surface with black dots (perithecia); lower surface bare, wrinkled, blackish at the center but brown toward the margin. Widespread on moist or wet rocks throughout North America. This lichen may form a distinct zone or band on rocks just above water level. It intergrades with *Dermatocarpon miniatum*, which is usually distinctly umbilicate, grows on drier rocks, and does not turn green when wet.

Figure 171.

164b Collected on dry rocks, never submerged; lobes flat and separate. 165

165a Black pycnidia along lobe margins; (use hand lens); lower surface tan to brown. Fig. 172. ....
....*Cetraria hepatizon* (Ach.) Vain.

Thallus dark brown, adnate, 4-8 cm broad; upper surface shiny, with conspicuous pycnidia; lower surface sparsely rhizinate; apothecia not common. Medulla K+ yellow→red, P+ orange (stictic acid). On exposed hard rocks in boreal regions or at high elevation southward. *Parmelia stygia* is very close but has laminal pycnidia (see below). On the whole these brown lichens are not well known and will present some problems.

Figure 172.

165b Pycnidia on the surface of lobes; lower surface mostly black. Fig. 173. ....*Parmelia stygia* (L.) Ach.

Figure 173.

Thallus dark brown or even blackish, adnate, 4-7 cm broad; upper surface shiny; lower surface sparsely rhizinate; apothecia not common. Medulla P+ red (fumarprotocetraric acid?). Widespread in arctic or boreal areas on exposed rocks. *Parmelia alpicola* Th. Fr., another arctic lichen, has narrower lobes (less than 1 mm) that are roughened and crowded.

166a Lower surface black (turning brown only at the margin). ..167

166b Lower surface uniformly tan to brown. 168

167a Upper surface and rim of apothecia smooth. Fig. 174. ....
....*Parmelia olivacea* (L.) Ach.

Figure 174.

Thallus brown to olive greenish brown, adnate, 3-7 cm broad; upper surface with tiny white pores (use high power lens); lower surface sparsely rhizinate; apothecia very common. Medulla P+ red (fumarprotocetraric acid). Common on deciduous trees and conifers in open woods or along roadsides. The old "*P. olivacea*" group has been split into several different species. In the Appalachians as far south as Alabama one will usually find *P. halei* Ahti, which has smaller fragile lobes with numerous lobules. Three species with a pale lower surface, *P. septentrionalis, P. trabeculata,* and *P. subolivacea,* are discussed below. *Parmelia glabra* (Schaer.) Nyl., known only from California, has minute hairs on the upper surface and reacts C+ red (lecanoric acid). A similar lichen without hairs in Colorado is probably undescribed. This whole group needs more study.

167b Upper surface and rim of apothecia with warts (use hand lens). Fig. 175. ....*Parmelia exasperata* **DeNot.**

Thallus dark brown, closely adnate, 2-4 cm broad; warts quite numerous, becoming subisidiate; lower surface moderately rhizinate; apothecia common. Widespread but never abundant on branches and trunks of trees in open woods or along roadsides. This lichen is most frequently collected in the southeastern states. In the northern states and Canada it may intergrade with *P. olivacea*. This lichen had previously been called *P. aspera*.

Figure 175.

168a Collected in western North America. Fig. 176. ....
....*Parmelia subolivacea* **Nyl.**

Thallus brown, closely adnate, 3-6 cm broad; lower surface brown or darkening, moderately rhizinate; apothecia common. Widespread on conifers and deciduous trees in open forests and along roadsides. This member of the "*P. olivacea*" group is distinguished by the P— color reaction and lack of white pores. *Parmelia multispora* Schneid. is virtually identical except that it has 16 spores per ascus. It occurs with *P. subolivacea* and all specimens must be sectioned for spores and examined under a microscope.

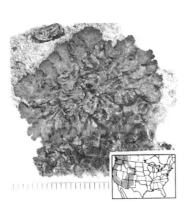

Figure 176.

168b Collected in eastern North America. 169

169a Lower surface bare or sparsely rhizinate (use low power lens). 170

169b Lower surface densely felty tomentose. 171

170a Apothecia present; lobes narrow and elongate. Fig. 177. ......
....*Parmelia septentrionalis* (Lynge) Ahti

Figure 177.

Thallus brown to olive or greenish brown, closely adnate, 2-6 cm broad; upper surface with some white pores (high power lens), shiny; lower surface light brown, rarely darkening, moderately rhizinate; apothecia numerous. Medulla P+ red (fumarprotocetraric acid). Common on trees in open woods, especially on alder, birch, and aspen. This species is especially common in the Great Lakes area and will usually be found in herbarium collections under the name "*P. olivacea.*" A rarer species in the boreal forests in Canada is *P. trabeculata* Ahti, which reacts K+ red (norstictic acid) and has a reticulate lower surface.

170b Apothecia lacking; lobes broader, short. Fig. 178. ....
................................*Dermatocarpon tuckermanii* (Rav.) Zahlbr.

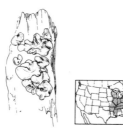

Figure 178.

Thallus light brown, adnate, 2-6 cm broad and composed of separate lobes (actually squamules) 3-6 mm long; lower surface brown, bare; upper surface with black dots (perithecia). Widespread but not commonly collected on deciduous trees, especially white oak, in open woods. This is the only species of *Dermatocarpon* in North America that grows on trees.

171a Thallus appressed; lobes about 1 mm wide. ....
...........................*Pannaria rubiginosa* (Ach.) Del. (see p. 108)

171b Thallus adnate to loosely attached; lobes 2-4 mm wide. ....
................................*Pannaria lurida* (Mont.) Nyl. (see p. 109)

172a Lobes narrow, 0.5-4.0 mm wide, linear to rotund (Fig. 179), usually adnate (but suberect in *Cetraria ciliaris* and *Platismatia* spp.). **173**

172b Lobes broader, 4-20 mm wide, irregular to rotund (Fig. 179), usually more loosely attached. ....216 (p. 118)

Figure 179. Lobe widths. Narrow and linear (left) and broad and rotund.

173a Thallus growing on tree bark or wood or mosses over bark. 174

173b Thallus growing on rocks, mosses over rocks, or soil. ....
....206 (p. 116)

174a Lower surface uniformly white, tan, brown, or mottled. 175

174b Lower surface black (sometimes turning brown in a narrow marginal zone) (lens needed for small specimens). ....
....194 (p. 109)

175a Margins of lobes with long cilia, 1-4 mm long (without lens).
....176

175b Cilia lacking (under lens some axillary cilia or projecting rhizines up to 0.5 mm long may be seen). 178

176a Thallus brownish mineral gray; collected in boreal localities. Fig. 180. ....*Anaptychia kaspica* Gyel.

Thallus loosely adnate, 4-8 cm broad; lower surface white, cortex lacking; apothecia not common. Common on rocks, especially along lake shores or the ocean, and at the base of trees in exposed areas such as sand dunes. The only similar lichen, *Physcia constipata* (see p. 118), has a lower cortex and rhizines.

Figure 180.

176b Thallus whitish mineral gray; collected in temperate or subtropical North Amercia. 177

177a Thallus lobes short and blunt, 2-3 cm long, tufted. Fig. 181. ....*Anaptychia echinata* (Tayl.) Kurok.

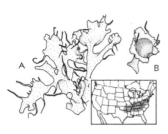

Thallus tufted and suberect, 2-3 cm broad; lower surface chalky white, the cortex lacking; apothecia numerous, the rim ciliate. Cortex K+ yellow (atranorin). Locally abundant on juniper twigs and other trees in open pastures. In southern California one will collect a related species, *Anaptychia erinacea* (Ach.) Trev., which has narrower lobes and grows on shrubs, cacti, and rocks in deserts.

Figure 181. A, thallus (X2); B, apothecium (X2).

177b Thallus lobes elongate, 3-8 cm long, subfruticose. ....
.... *Anaptychia leucomelaena* (see p. 50)

178a Lower surface white and cottony (use high power lens), cortex lacking. 179

178b Lower surface whitish to tan, not cottony, cortex and rhizines present. 180

179a Thallus lacking lobules or only sparsely lobulate; apothecia common. Fig. 182. .... *Anaptychia hypoleuca* (Muhl.) Mass.

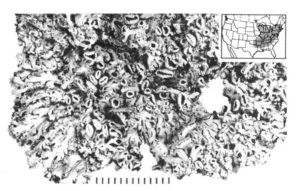

Figure 182.

Thallus whitish mineral gray, adnate, 3-6 cm broad; lobe margins and rim of apothecia becoming sparsely lobulate with age; lower surface with short marginal rhizines; apothecia common. Cortex K+ yellow (atranorin). Rather rare on deciduous trees in open woods or along roadsides. There is some intergradation with *A. squamulosa* (below) but the lobules are more appressed rather than erect.

179b Lobes densely squamulose; apothecia rare. Fig. 183. ....
....*Anaptychia squamulosa* **Degel.**

Thallus whitish mineral gray, adnate, 3-8 cm broad, often coalescing into extensive colonies; lower surface with scattered marginal rhizines; apothecia rare. Cortex K+ yellow (atranorin). Common at the base of oak trees in open woods in the Appalachians.

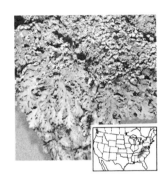

Figure 183.

180a Lobes in general narrow and linear, 1-3 mm wide. 181

180b Lobes broader, irregular and apically rotund, 3-6 mm wide.
....**192**

181a Upper surface and margins of lobes squamulose. 182

181b Squamules lacking. 183

182a Squamules appressed; apothecia common, the rim squamulose. Fig. 184. ....*Anaptychia palmatula* (**Michx.**) **Vain.**
Thallus light brownish mineral gray, turning deep green when wet, adnate, 4-8 cm broad; lower surface whitish or light tan, moderately rhizinate; apothecia very numerous. Cortex K+ yellow (atranorin) or K–. Common at the base of deciduous trees and on shaded rocks in closed woods. *Physcia lacinulata* is close but has more irregular erect squamules.

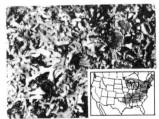

Figure 184.

182b Squamules erect; apothecia rare, the rim without squamules. Fig. 185. ....*Physcia lacinulata* **Müll. Arg.**

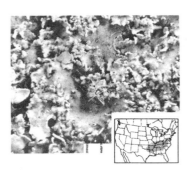

Figure 185.

Thallus greenish or brownish mineral gray, adnate, 4-8 cm broad; upper surface sometimes becoming white pruinose; lower surface white, densely rhizinate; apothecia rare. Common at the base of deciduous trees in closed woods. If the lobules are poorly developed, it might be mistaken for *Physcia ciliata*, which has a dark lower surface and is more closely appressed. *Parmeliella pannosa* (see p. 112), a Coastal Plain species, has similar lobules but is densely tomentose below.

183a Thallus suberect, easily detached from the substratum by hand. 184

183b Thallus closely attached, removed only with a knife. 186

184a Lower surface with a distinct channel (see Fig. 403). ....
.................................*Pseudevernia intensa* **(see p. 198)**

184b Lower surface flat, not channelled. 185

185a Lobes elongate, often curled up at the edges. Fig. 186. ....
.........................*Platismatia stenophylla* **(Tuck.) Culb. & Culb.**

Figure 186.

Thallus light mineral gray to brownish, loosely attached, 6-12 cm broad; upper surface smooth to wrinkled; lower surface wrinkled, bare, blackening at the center but tan to mottled white at the margins; apothecia rare. Cortex K+ yellow (atranorin). Common on exposed trees. *Platismatia herrei* (see p. 79) is very close but produces marginal isidia; *P. glauca* (see p. 70) has broader lobes and soredia.

185b Lobes shorter and irregular, flat. ....
.................................*Cetraria ciliaris* **(see p. 97)**

186a Medulla pale yellow-orange (section with razor blade). ....
.... *Parmelia congruens* (see p. 95)

186b Medulla white. 187

187a Cortex K+ yellow. 188

187b Cortex K— (turning greenish after a few minutes). Fig. 187.
....*Physcia pulverulenta* (Schreb.) Hampe

Thallus whitish mineral gray,
sometimes turning brownish, adnate,
3-6 cm broad; upper surface finely
scabrid and pruinose, some lobules
developing; lower surface buff to
dark brown, moderately rhizinate;
apothecia common. Rather rare on
trees in open woods or along roadsides. This lichen is close to *Physcia
grisea* but lacks soredia. The pruinose cortex and K— test will separate it from *P. aipolia.* The western
collections are often blackish below.

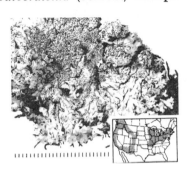

Figure 187.

188a Apothecia 0.5-2.0 mm wide, narrower than the lobes; usually
collected on hardwood trees. 189

188b Apothecia up to 6 mm wide, broader than the lobes; usually
collected on conifers. Fig. 188. ....
....*Parmeliopsis placorodia* (Ach.) Nyl.

Thallus whitish gray green, adnate,
2-4 cm broad; lower surface white,
moderately rhizinate; apothecia numerous. Cortex and medulla K+ yellow, P+ yellow (thamnolic acid).
Locally abundant in scrub pine forests
and along roadsides. This species often
grows with *Cetraria aurescens* and *Parmeliopsis aleurites* on dead branches.

Figure 188. (X2).

189a Thallus whitish mineral gray; lower surface moderately rhizinate (use hand lens). 190

189b Thallus light brownish; lower surface tan, densely tomen-
tose. 191

190a Upper surface continuous; rhizines uniformly white (use hand lens); medulla K—. Fig. 189. .... *Physcia stellaris* (L.) Nyl.

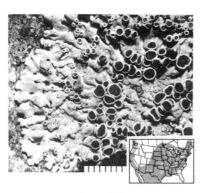

Thallus closely adnate, 2-4 cm broad; below sparsely to moderately rhizinate; apothecia very common. Cortex K+ yellow (atranorin). Very common on deciduous trees, more rarely on conifers, in open woods or along roadsides. This species often grows in the canopy on small branches, while closely related *Physcia aipolia,* which has white spots, grows more toward the base. A KOH test is needed to tell these two apart. Certain western collections, sometimes on rock, are known as *P. biziana* (Mass.) Zahlbr. and *P. albinea*

Figure 189.

(Ach.) Nyl. but are probably not distinguishable from *P. stellaris.*

190b Upper surface strongly white-spotted (use hand lens); rhizines darkening; medulla K+ yellow. Fig. 190. ....

.... *Physcia aipolia* (Ehrh.) Hampe

Thallus closely adnate, 3-6 cm broad; lower surface white with moderate to dense darkish rhizines, often projecting beyond the margin; apothecia very common. Cortex and medulla K+ yellow (atranorin). Extremely common on exposed deciduous trees and often collected on roadside trees in small towns. The thallus is thicker than in *Physcia stellaris* in addition to the differences in K test and white-spotting. From North Carolina to Texas it intergrades with *P. alba* (Fée) Müll. Arg., which has smaller lobes (less than 1 mm) but is otherwise very close.

Figure 190.

191a Lobes adnate, crowded, 1-2 mm wide. Fig. 191. ....

.... *Pannaria rubiginosa* (Ach.) Del.

Thallus light brownish gray, closely adnate, 2-5 cm broad; upper surface sometimes white pruinose toward the margins, becoming short lobulate; lower surface variable, tan to dark brown, densely tomentose; algae blue-green; apothecia common. Widespread on rocks and the base of deciduous trees in mature forests. *Pannaria lurida* (below) has much broader lobes and reacts P+ red. *Pannaria leucosticta* has smaller squamulate lobes and denser pruina.

Figure 191.

191b Lobes more loosely attached, 2-4 mm wide. Fig. 192. ....
....*Pannaria lurida* (Mont.) Nyl.

Thallus dull brownish, 4-6 cm broad; lower surface buff, with long conspicuous tomentum; algae blue-green; apothecia common. Medulla P+ orange red (pannarin) or rarely P–. On oaks and junipers in exposed woods, near cliffs, or at the base of trees along roadsides. This species is not often collected but is easily recognized by the tomentum. *Pannaria rubiginosa* (above) intergrades with it but is usually smaller and more adnate.

Figure 192.

192a Upper cortex and rim of apothecia with white pores............
....*Parmelia bolliana* (see p. 123)

192b White pores lacking. 193

193a Lobes deeply wrinkled (without lens); thallus greenish mineral gray. ....*Lobaria erosa* (see p. 124)

193b Lobes plane; thallus brownish gray. ....
.... *Nephroma helveticum* (see p. 98)

194a Lobes 1-4 mm wide, adnate, loosely attached, or suberect.
....195

194b Lobes narrow and appressed to subcrustose, 0.3-1.0 mm wide.
....203

195a **Lobes hollow (section with razor blade), appearing round and inflated. Fig. 193.** ......*Hypogymnia enteromorpha* **(Ach.) Nyl.**

Thallus light mineral gray, adnate to suberect, 5-10 cm broad; lower surface black, wrinkled; apothecia common. Cortex K+ yellow (atranorin); medulla P+ red (physodalic acid) or P−. On branches and trunks of conifers in open forests. The eastern form (higher elevations of the Appalachians) has rather narrow lobes (1.0-1.5 mm), whereas the typical western form is twice this. In arctic-alpine habitats one will collect *H. subobscura* (Vain.) Poelt., which has an unusual

Figure 193.

brown-black reticulate upper surface and is P−. Three western or arctic-alpine species appear similar but have a solid medulla: *H. encausta* (Sm.) W. Wats., which is brownish and P+ red; *H. intestiniformis* (Vill.) Räs., very dark mineral gray and P−; and *Cavernularia lophyrea* (Ach.) Degel., which has deep pores as in *C. hultenii*.

195b **Lobes solid, usually flat (inflated in** *Anzia***).** 196

196a **Collected in California. Fig. 194.** ....
....*Parmelia quercina* **(Willd.) Vain.**

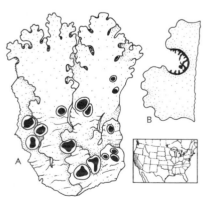

Thallus light mineral gray, adnate, 3-10 cm broad; lower surface black and densely rhizinate, with some cilia in lobe axils; apothecia common. Cortex K+ yellow (atranorin); medulla C+, KC+ red (lecanoric acid). Common on oak trees. Reports of this species from eastern North America have been based on *Parmelia galbina* or *P. livida* (see p. 113).

Figure 194. A, thallus (X2); B, axil with short cilia (X5).

199a Tomentum spongy, breaking away and leaving white spots; lobes appearing inflated. Fig. 195. ....
................*Anzia colpodes* (Ach.) Stizb.

Thallus light mineral gray, leathery, adnate, 3-7 cm broad; pycnidia common on upper surface; apothecia common, spores tiny (1 micron), numerous in each ascus. Cortex K+ yellow (atranorin); divaricatic acid present in medulla. Widespread on deciduous trees, especially red oak and hickory. This species is probably overlooked because it grows in tree tops. Superficially it looks like a species of *Hypogymnia*, but the lobes are solid.

Figure 195.

199b Tomentum simple, projecting beyond lobe margins; lobes flat. 200

200a Thallus slate-blue to dark mineral gray. Fig. 196. ....
................*Coccocarpia parmelioides* (Hook.) Curt.

Thallus adnate, 3-6 cm broad; lower surface black to deep gray, densely tomentose; algae blue-green; apothecia common, the disc black. Widespread on deciduous trees in open forests or along roadsides. This species, closely related to isidiate *Coccocarpia cronia* (p. 81), is most common in Florida.

Figure 196.

200b Thallus mineral to brownish gray. Fig. 197. ....
....*Parmeliella pannosa* (Sw.) Nyl.

Figure 197.

Thallus closely adnate, 4-8 cm broad, rather fragile; marginal tomentum conspicuous; upper surface becoming squamulose; algae blue-green; apothecia usually lacking. Rather rare on deciduous trees in mature woods. This is a tropical species that is apparently disappearing as the forests are cut down. Another species in this genus, *P. plumbea* (Lightf.) Müll. Arg., has a much larger thallus; it is rarely collected on trees and rocks from Maine to Nova Scotia.

201a Medulla K+ yellow→ red; rhizines simple (use high power lens). Fig. 198. ....*Parmelia galbina* Ach.

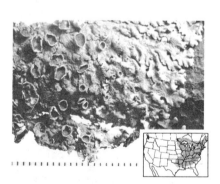

Figure 198.

Thallus greenish mineral gray, closely adnate, 3-10 cm broad; upper surface becoming finely wrinkled with numerous small black dots (pycnidia); margins short-ciliate, especially in the axils; medulla pale yellow orange, at least beneath apothecia; apothecia very common. Cortex K+ yellow (atranorin); medulla K+ yellow→ red, P+ orange (galbinic acid). Very common on trunks and branches of deciduous trees in open forests. *Parmelia livida* (see below) has been confused with this species but has different rhizines and chemistry.

201b Medulla K— or K+ faint yellow; rhizines branched (use high power lens). Fig. 199. ....*Parmelia livida* **Tayl.**

Thallus whitish mineral gray, closely adnate, 4-9 cm broad; lower surface moderately rhizinate; apothecia very common. Cortex K+ yellow (atranorin); medulla KC+ rose (4-0-methyl physodic acid and lividic acid). Common on trunks and branches of deciduous trees in open woods or along roadsides. An almost identical species, *Parmelia pulvinata* Fée, occurs on trees in southern Arizona and New Mexico; it contains evernic

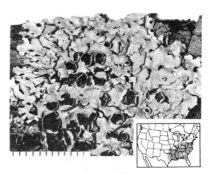

Figure 199.

acid. At high elevations in Virginia and North Carolina one may find *P. virginica* Hale, which has a roughened almost pustulate cortex and KC+ orange reaction (barbatic acid).

202a Upper surface becoming densely squamulose; cortex with white pores (use lens). Fig. 200. ....
............................*Parmelia appalachensis* **Culb.**

Thallus greenish mineral gray, adnate, 6-10 cm broad; upper surface wrinkled, pores sparse and inconspicuous; lower surface sparsely rhizinate; apothecia not common. Cortex K+ yellow (atranorin); protolichesterinic acid also in the medulla. Common at the base of oak trees in open woods. The black lower surface separates this species from the other pseudocyphellate Parmelias, *P. bolliana* and *P. rudecta*.

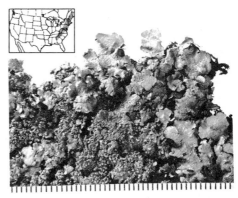

Figure 200.

202b Squamules and white pores lacking. Fig. 201. ....
....*Parmelia michauxiana* **Zahlbr.**

Figure 201.

Thallus whitish mineral gray, adnate, 4-12 cm broad; pycnidia numerous on the upper surface; lobe axils with short cilia; lower surface moderately rhizinate; apothecia very common, somewhat stalked. Cortex K+ yellow (atranorin); medulla P+ red (protocetraric acid). Common on trunks and branches in open woods and along roadsides. The lobe margins may become quite dissected and laciniate. It might be confused with *Parmelia cetrata,* which has a strongly reticulate cortex and K+ red reaction. In southern Florida, a rare lichen with protocetraric acid, *P. zollingeri* Hepp, is distinguished by much broader rotund lobes (up to 20 mm) and lack of any cilia.

203a Lobe margins with short inflated cilia (use high power lens).
Fig. 202. ....*Parmelia confoederata* **Culb.**

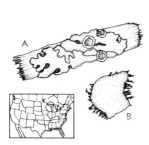

Figure 202. A, thallus (X4); bulbate cilia (X20).

Thallus whitish mineral gray, appressed, 2-5 cm broad; lower surface black, densely rhizinate, the rhizines branched; apothecia common, the rim covered with black dots (pycnidia). Cortex K+ yellow (atranorin); medulla C+, KC + red (lecanoric acid). Common in exposed scrub forests on twigs and branches. This species is easily overlooked because of the small size. Another species with inflated cilia, *Parmelia coronata* Fée, reacts C+ rose (gyrophoric acid) and has been collected in western Texas.

203b Lobe margins without cilia (but with fine colorless hairs in
**   *Physcia ciliata*).** **204**

204a Thallus brownish mineral gray; lobes separate. **205**

204b Thallus whitish mineral gray; lobes crowded and appearing
**   fused. Fig. 203.** ....*Dirinaria aegialita* (**Ach.**) **Moore**

Thallus closely appressed, 4-10 cm broad; lower surface black and naked (hard to determine in most specimens); apothecia very common. Cortex K+ yellow (atranorin); divaricatic or sekikaic acids also present. Common on exposed trees, rarely on rocks. *Dirinaria purpurascens* (Vain.) Moore is extremely close but is separated by apothecia with a red or purple interior (section with razor blade). Several

Figure 203.

rare species of *Pyxine*, most of them in Florida, will key out here. Imshaug's study (1957) should be consulted, along with Moore's flora (1968).

205a Lower surface black; lobes 0.5-1.0 mm wide, often with fine hairs on the upper surface and apothecia. Fig. 204. ....
....*Physcia ciliata* **(Hoffm.) DR.**

Thallus dark mineral or brownish gray, closely adnate, 2-3 cm broad; lower surface densely rhizinate; apothecia common. Widespread on deciduous trees, especially aspen, in exposed or open woods and along roadsides. About half of the specimens will have hairs and are called forma *fibrillosa*. Robust specimens resemble *Physcia stellaris*, which differs in having a white lower surface and K+ yellow reaction. *Physcia syncolla* (below) is much more closely appressed.

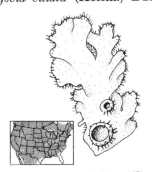

Figure 204. Thallus (X5).

205b Lower surface dark to brown; lobes 0.5 mm wide or less, closely appressed; hairs always lacking. Fig. 205. ....
....*Physcia syncolla* **Tuck.**

Thallus 1-2 cm broad; lower surface sparsely rhizinate (difficult to determine in most specimens); apothecia common. Widespread in deciduous forests but most common on isolated trees in the prairie-forest states (Minnesota to Texas). It is easily overlooked because it blends with the bark. Rarely the medulla will be orange.

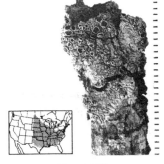

Figure 205.

206a Lower surface black (difficult to determine in appressed
     Dirinaria aegialita), turning brown only at the margin. 207

206b Lower surface uniformly tan, brown, or white. 210

207a Upper cortex ridged and with white markings (use low power
     lens). Fig. 206. ....*Parmelia omphalodes* (L.) Ach.

Thallus greenish or whitish mineral gray to brown, loosely adnate,
6-15 cm broad; lower surface black
and moderately rhizinate; apothecia
common. Cortex K+ yellow (atranorin); medulla K+ yellow→red, P+
orange (salacinic acid). Widespread
on exposed boulders in open areas
and talus slopes. This is a common
lichen on rocks in arctic and alpine
localities and could only be confused
with *Parmelia saxatilis* (see p. 80),
which has coarse isidia.

Figure 206.

207a Upper cortex not ridged, without white markings. 208

208a Collected in the Coastal Plain and Piedmont of the southern
     United States. ....*Dirinaria aegialita* (see p. 114)

208b Collected in boreal or mountainous areas of North America
    209

209a Upper cortex scabrid and white pruinose. Fig. 207. ....
     ....*Physcia muscigena* (Ach.) Nyl.

Thallus dark mineral gray to light
brown, often with a whitish cast, adnate,
4-10 cm broad; upper surface with a
raised whitish rim along the margins;
lower surface densely rhizinate; apothecia
rare. Common over mosses on soil and
over rocks in exposed areas.

Figure 207.

209b Upper cortex smooth, without pruina. Fig. 208. ....
....*Physcia endococcinea* (**Körb.**) **Th. Fr.**

Thallus mineral gray, adnate,
2-5 cm broad; lower surface densely rhizinate; apothecia common.
Rare on sheltered rocks. The medulla is usually white but a form
with an orange medulla will also
be collected. The species is very
close to *Physcia ciliata* (see p.
115).

Figure 208.

210a Lobe margins with conspicuous cilia, 1-3 mm long (do not use
lens). ....*Anaptychia kaspica* (see p. 103)

210b Lobe margins without cilia (projecting rhizines or sparse cilia
may measure up to 0.5 mm using lens). 211

211a Lobes 2-5 mm wide; upper cortex with white pores (low
power lens). ....*Parmelia bolliana* (see p. 123)

211b Lobes narrower, 0.3-2.0 mm wide; pores lacking. 212

212a Thallus squamulose, turning green when wet. ....
.... ,,....*Anaptychia palmatula* (see p. 105)

212b Thallus not squamulose (without lens) or turning green when
wet. 213

213a Lobes very narrow, 0.3-0.6 mm wide. Fig. 209. ....
....*Physcia halei* **Thoms.**

Thallus whitish mineral gray, closely
adnate, scattered, 2-3 cm broad; lower
surface white, moderately rhizinate;
apothecia common. Cortex and medulla K+ yellow (usually difficult to
tell) (atranorin). Widespread on granite and sandstone in open areas. Some
specimens of *Physcia subtilis* (see p.
48) will key here if the soredia are
sparse or overlooked. *Physcia phaea*
(below) is much larger and has white
spotting.

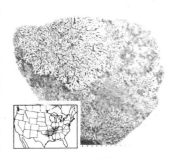

Figure 209.

213b Lobes broader, 1-2 mm wide. 214

214a Upper cortex with distinct white spotting (use low power
    lens). Fig. 210. ....Physcia phaea (Tuck.) Thoms.

Thallus whitish mineral gray, adnate,
2-5 cm broad; lower surface white,
moderately rhizinate; apothecia numerous. Cortex and medulla K+ yellow
(atranorin). Fairly common on sheltered rocks in open woods. It is ob-
viously related to Physcia aipolia, a
common bark species.

Figure 210.

214b Upper cortex not white spotted. 215

215a Lower surface sparsely rhizinate (use lower power lens). Fig.
    211. ....Physcia constipata (Norrl.) Nyl.

Thallus light brownish gray, adnate,
3-7 cm broad; lower surface buff, marginal rhizines projecting out from up-
turned lobe tips; apothecia rare. Rather
rare on soil in open forests or among
rocks. This species might be confused
with Anaptychia kaspica (see p. 103),
which has long cilia and lacks a lower
cortex.

Figure 211. Thallus (X2) and
lobe tips (X5).

215b Lower surface tomentose. ....Pannaria rubiginosa (see p. 108)

216a Margins of lobes with black cilia, 1-2 mm long (use hand
    lens). 217

216b Margins of lobes without cilia. 219

217a Lower surface with a black center and conspicuous white rim
    at the margin (without lens). Fig. 212. ....
    ....Parmelia perforata (Jacq.) Ach.

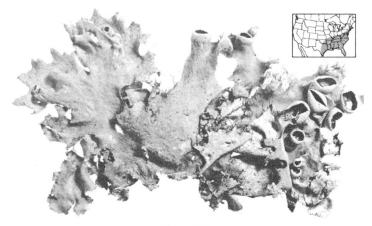

Figure 212.

Thallus whitish mineral gray, loosely attached to subcrect, 6-12 cm broad; upper surface faintly white-spotted (use high power lens); lower surface bare to sparsely rhizinate; apothecia common, stalked and with a hole in the disc. Cortex K+ yellow (atranorin); medulla K+ yellow→red, P+ orange (norstictic and protolichesterinic acids). Common on branches at the tops of trees and on exposed trunks. *Parmelia rigida* Lynge, a chemical variant with alectoronic acid (K−, KC+ red), occurs with this species from coastal North Carolina to Texas. A chemical test must be made to separate them.

217b Lower surface more or less uniformly black, brown only at the lobe margins. 218

218a Upper cortex reticulately cracked to the margin (see Fig. 5A) (use hand lens); rhizines dense below. Fig. 213. ....
....*Parmelia cetrata* Ach.

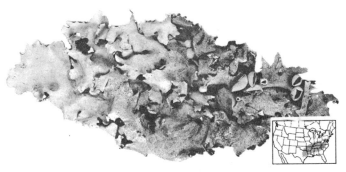

Figure 213.

Thallus light mineral gray (often turning reddish after pressing and drying), adnate, 6-12 cm broad; lobes often laciniate; cilia rather inconspicuous; lower surface densely rhizinate but with a narrow marginal zone; apothecia common, the disc with a central hole. Cortex K+ yellow (atranorin); medulla K+ yellow→red, P+ orange (salacinic acid). Widespread on deciduous trees in open woods or pastures. This is the nonsorediate phase of *Parmelia reticulata* (see p. 65). *Parmelia perforata* also has perforate apothecia but the lower surface is different.

218b **Upper cortex continuous; rhizines sparse or lacking.** ....
.... *Cetraria ciliaris* (see p. 97)

219a **Upper surface broadly reticulately ridged (without hand lens).** 220

219b **Upper surface smooth to plane or wrinkled.** 222

220a **Lower surface bare and shiny, white or black and white mottled.** 221

220b **Lower surface tan and white mottled, felty. Fig. 214.**...........
.... *Lobaria linita* (Ach.) Rabh.

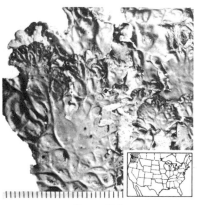

Thallus light greenish or brownish mineral gray, loosely attached, 6-15 cm broad; apothecia common. Tenuiorin in the medulla. Common in open forests or among large boulders. *Lobaria pulmonaria* is the same size but is sorediate. These two conspicuous lichens may occur together.

Figure 214.

221a **Collected in eastern North America. Fig. 215.** ....
.....................*Platismatia tuckermanii* (Oakes) Culb. & Culb.

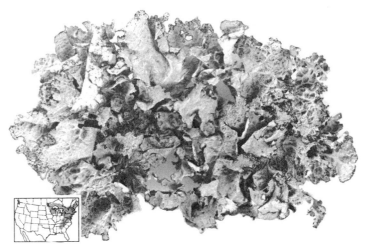

Figure 215.

Thallus mineral gray to whitish, loosely adnate to suberect, 4-10 cm broad; lower surface white and black or brown mottled, sparsely rhizinate or bare; apothecia common. Cortex K+ yellow (atranorin); protolichesterinic acid also present in medulla. Common on branches and trunks of conifers in open woods. *Cetraria ciliaris* grows with this lichen very frequently and they should be carefully distinguished. Usually *C. ciliaris* has narrower brownish lobes and some marginal cilia with only weak ridging on the upper surface.

221b Collected in western North America. Fig. 216. ....
........................*Platismatia lacunosa* **(Ach.) Culb. & Culb.**

Thallus mineral gray or whitish, loosely adnate, 4-10 cm broad; ridges sharp and distinct; lower surface white and black or brown mottled, bare; apothecia common. Cortex K+ yellow (atranorin); medulla P+ red (fumarprotocetraric acid). Fairly common on exposed conifers. The sharp ridges and geography separate this from *Platismatia tuckermanii.*

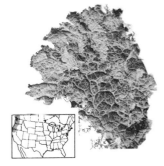

Figure 216.

222a Lower surface orange or cinnabar red (without lens); collected in arctic and western North America. Fig. 217. ....
....*Solorina crocea* (L.) Ach.

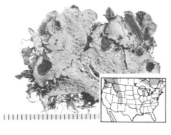

Figure 217.

Thallus light greenish brown, adnate, 4-6 cm broad; medulla orange red; lower surface lacking a cortex but with distinct veins; apothecia common, located in sunken pits on the surface. Medulla K+ purple (solorinic acid). Common on soil. This unusual arctic lichen cannot be mistaken for any other species.

222b Lower surface not orange; collected in boreal or temperate North America. 223

223a Apothecia immersed in pits on the upper surface. Fig. 218. ....*Solorina saccata* (L.) Ach.

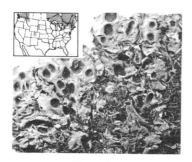

Figure 218.

Thallus greenish or brownish mineral gray, adnate, 3-6 cm broad; upper surface turning white pruinose; lower surface tan, without a cortex; apothecia common, the asci with 4 brown spores. Rare on soil or over mosses in open woods. Two nearly identical species in western North America are separated by spore number: *S. bispora* Nyl. has two large brown spores and *S. octospora* Arn. has eight. All western specimens in this genus should be sectioned and examined with a microscope.

223b Apothecia adnate to stalked or lacking. 224

224a Lower surface black, turning brown only at the margin. 225

224b Lower surface uniformly brown or mottled brown and white. 227

225a Upper surface densely squamulose. ....
....*Parmelia appalachensis* (see p. 113)

225b Upper surface without squamules. 226

226a Lower surface with dense black tomentum. ....
....*Coccocarpia parmelioides* (see p. 111)

226b Lower surface with sparse rhizines. ....
....*Parmelia michauxiana* (see p. 114)

227a Upper surface of lobes and margins of apothecia with white
pores (use hand lens). Fig. 219. ...*Parmelia bolliana* Müll. Arg.

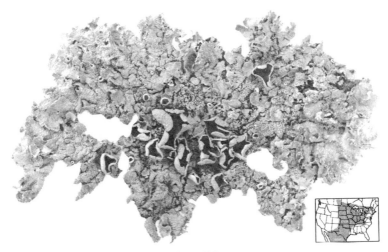

Figure 219.

Thallus greenish mineral gray, adnate, 6-12 cm broad; upper surface becoming quite wrinkled, often lobulate with age; white pores
inconspicuous; lower surface tan with moderate rhizines; black
pores (pycnidia) (see Fig. 14C) and apothecia common. Cortex
K+ yellow (atranorin); medulla C+, KC+ red (lecanoric acid)
or C−, KC− (protolichesterinic acid). Common on trunks of exposed deciduous trees. The C+ red variant is called *Parmelia
hypoleucites* Nyl.; it occurs on trees intermingled with the C− variant as well as on rocks in open areas, mainly from southern Minnesota southward.

227b Upper surface without white pores. 228

228a Lobes rather narrow and loosely attached to suberect; marginal black pycnidia common. ....
.... *Cetraria ciliaris* (see p. 97)

228b Lobes broader and more closely attached; pycnidia laminal
or lacking. 229

229a Lobes 6-15 mm wide, leathery; collected in Canada and the northeastern states south to the Piedmont. Fig. 220. ....
....*Lobaria quercizans* **Michx.**

Thallus light brownish mineral gray, turning bright green when wet, 6-20 cm broad; lower surface tan, felty, with some tufts of tomentum; apothecia common. Medulla C+, KC+ rose (gyrophoric acid). Common on deciduous trees, especially maples, in open woods and swamps, and on rocks. This conspicuous lichen will at first be confused with *Parmelia*, but the lower surface is tan and felty rather than rhizinate.

Figure 220. (X1/2).

229b Lobes 2-5 mm wide, fragile; collected in southeastern United States in the Coastal Plain and Piedmont. Fig. 221. ....
....*Lobaria erosa* **(Eschw.) Nyl.**

Thallus greenish or brownish mineral gray, adnate, 4-8 cm broad; upper surface wrinkled, often developing squamules; lower surface tan, bare or with tufted tomentum; apothecia common. Medulla C+, KC+ red (gyrophoric acid). On deciduous trees, especially beech, in mature or closed forests. Where their ranges overlap from North Carolina to Arkansas, *Lobaria erosa* and *L. quercizans* are separated mostly on size.

Figure 221.

II. Gelatinous Lichens

These lichens always contain a blue-green alga, usually *Nostoc*, scattered through the thallus. The thallus is black to dark bluish or slate mineral gray. The species are often collected at the base of trees in moist woods and some typically grow on rocks and soil. It is a variable and difficult group, however, with much intergradation between species, and except for *Leptogium* (see Sierk, 1964) they are very poorly known. Spore characters are important in *Collema*, and microscopic examination will be necessary in many cases. None of the gelatinous lichens, unfortunately, has useful chemical reactions.

1a Collected submerged in mountain streams. Fig. 222. ....
.... *Hydrotheria venosa* **Russell**

Thallus bluish to brownish mineral gray, 4-6 cm broad, very fragile when dry; lower surface veined, the veins light brown; apothecia common. Rarely collected in mountainous areas. This is one of the few truly aquatic foliose lichens. It looks like a large *Leptogium*. Actually *Leptogium rivale* Tuck., known in Colorado and Wyoming, is semi-aquatic but is less than 2 cm broad.

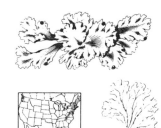

Figure 222.

1b Collected on dry rocks, trees, or soil. 2

2a Upper surface or margins with squamiform, globular, or cylindrical isidia (use hand lens). 3

2b Upper surface without isidia. (Margins finely dissected in *Leptogium lichenoides*). 8

3a Lower surface with dense whitish tomentum. Fig. 223. ....
.... *Leptogium hirsutum* **Sierk**

Thallus deep mouse gray, loosely adnate, 3-10 cm broad; upper surface moderately isidiate; apothecia very rare. This is the commonest species in the United States of a group that includes *L. saturninum* (Dicks.) Nyl., which has granular isidia and a northern and western distribution, and *L. americanum* Degel., which has very short tomentum (less than 100μ) of spherical rather than cylindrical cells and occurs rather rarely in New England, New York, and the southern Appalachians. *L. fur-*

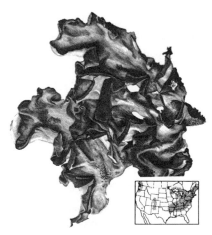

Figure 223.

furaceum (Harm.) Sierk lacks tomentum on the upper surface, is brownish, and occurs only in the western states.

3b **Lower surface bare, usually the same color as the upper surface, tomentum lacking (rarely with isolated tufts of attachment hairs).** **4**

4a **Apothecia and/or isidia in regular rows along margins or ridges of lobes. Fig. 224.** ....*Leptogium marginellum* (Sw.) S. Gray

Figure 224.

Thallus bluish gray, adnate, 4-6 cm broad; upper surface finely wrinkled; margins sparsely to moderately isidiate, the isidia simple, often associated with numerous apothecia with tan rim. Fairly common on deciduous trees in open woods or along roadsides. *Leptogium isidosellum* (Ridd.) Sierk, a species occurring only in Florida, has cylindrical branched isidia along the ridges and usually lacks apothecia.

4b **Apothecia lacking or if present mostly laminal; isidia scattered.** **5**

5a **Thallus bluish or brownish slate-colored or dark mineral gray; upper surface smooth or wrinkled (under hand lens), at least in part shiny.** **6**

5b Thallus blackish brown or olive black to black; upper surface
smooth or pustulate, dull. 7

6a Upper surface plane, without wrinkles (use hand lens). Fig. 225.
....*Leptogium cyanescens* (Ach.) Körb.

Thallus bluish slate-colored,
adnate, 3-7 cm broad; upper
surface densely isidiate; apothecia very rare. This is probably the most commonly collected *Leptogium* in the
deciduous forests of North
America, but it can easily be
confused in the South with
L. austroamericanum, which
has a wrinkled upper cortex.
A species more common
on limestone, *L. dactylinum*
Tuck., has a smaller olivace-
ous thallus and numerous
apothecia. A species with squamiform isidia, *L. denticulatum* Nyl.,
occurs on rocks from Colorado southward in the western states.

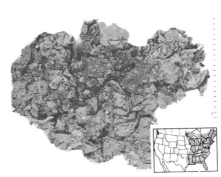

Figure 225.

6b Upper surface wrinkled and rugose. Fig. 226. ....
............................*Leptogium austroamericanum* (Malme) Dodge

Thallus bluish gray, adnate,
2-6 cm broad, often crowded;
upper surface densely isidiate,
dull; apothecia very rare. Common on deciduous trees in
open dry woods. Within its
range, this species is as common as *L. cyanescens* but is
distinct because of the thicker,
wrinkled thallus. A western
species, *L. arsenei* Sierk, has a
very thick thallus, 200-500μ.
L. millegranum Sierk has fused
overlapping lobes and closely
resembles *L. chloromelum* except for isidia; it has widespread occurrence in temperate North America.

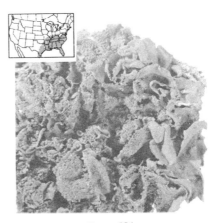

Figure 226.

7a Collected on trees. Fig. 227. ....

....*Collema subfurvum* (Müll. Arg.) Degel.

Figure 227.

Thallus deep olive brown to black, adnate, 4-8 cm broad; upper surface plane to undulating, the isidia dense, globose; lower surface naked, light olive brown; apothecia rare, the spores transversely septate. Very common at the base of trees in open forests and along roadsides. This lichen intergrades with *C. furfuraceum* (Arn.) DR., a widespread but rarer corticolous lichen with a pustulate upper surface and thin cylindrical isidia on the pustules. *C. subfurfuraceum* Degel., also pustulate, has a pruinose apothecial disc but is known rarely only in Florida.

7b Collected on rocks or soil. Fig. 228. ....

....*Collema flaccidum* (Ach.) Ach.

Figure 228.

Thallus olive green to dark brown, adnate, 4-8 cm broad; upper surface finely isidiate, becoming lobulate-isidiate with age; lower surface naked, wrinkled, greenish or olive gray; apothecia not common, the spores transversely septate. On limey rocks in fairly sheltered areas, rarely on trees. Other isidiate saxicolous or soil-inhabiting species, all of them very difficult to separate, include *C. tunaeforme* Ach. with muriform spores, *C. crispum* (Huds.) Wigg. with 4-celled spores, and *C. cristatum* (L.) Wigg. with submuriform spores. These will be found mostly in the western states. *Leptogium plicatile* (Ach.) Leight. will also key out here; it has a small thallus (1-2 cm.), with short plicate lobes, and muriform spores.

8a Collected on trees or on mosses over bark. (*Leptogium corticola* rarely also on rocks). 9

8b Collected on rocks, soil, or growing over mosses on rocks or the base of trees. 14

9a Thallus bluish to brownish gray or slate-colored, the surface shiny. 10

9b Thallus black to blackish brown, the surface dull. 12

10a Lobes overlapping, appearing to fuse together, irregular in outline, forming a compact more or less radiating thallus. Fig. 229. ....*Leptogium chloromelum* (Ach.) Nyl.

Figure 229.

Thallus dark brownish mineral gray, closely adnate, 3-7 cm broad; upper surface deeply wrinkled; lower surface wrinkled; apothecia not common. Common on deciduous trees in open woods. *Leptogium phyllocarpum* (Pers.) Mont. differs in having lobulate growths on the apothecia and a bluish gray color; it occurs from coastal North Carolina southward in the Gulf region. In Florida there are three other similar species: *L. stipitatum* Vain., with apothecia borne on hollow inflated lobes, *L. sessile* Vain. with orbicular lobes, and *L. floridanum* Sierk with thick warty lobes.

10b Lobes broad and flattened, separate, usually rotund. 11

11a Surface of lobes finely wrinkled (use hand lens). Fig. 230. ......
....*Leptogium corticola* Tayl.

Thallus bluish slate gray, adnate, 3-8 cm broad; upper surface shiny; lower surface slate gray; apothecia numerous over the surface. Widespread on the base of deciduous trees or on rocks in mature forests, never abundant but easily recognized at sight.

Figure 230.

11b Surface of lobes smooth to finely pitted. Fig. 231. ....
....*Leptogium azureum* (Sw.) Mont.

Figure 231.

Thallus light bluish lead-colored, adnate, 4-8 cm broad; upper
surface shiny; lower surface bluish gray; apothecia common. Rather
rare on bark of trees in closed woods. *Leptogium cyanescens* is very
close in color and habit but has isidia; *L. microstictum* Vain., known
only from Florida, has a pitted upper surface. A rarely collected
species in eastern North America, *L. crenatellum* Tuck., grows on
trees near swamps where it is periodically inundated.

12a Upper surface pustulate (without hand lens); thallus expanded,
     3-6 cm broad. Fig. 232. ....*Collema nigrescens* (Huds.) DC.

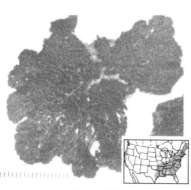

Figure 232.

Thallus dark brown, closely
adnate, 3-6 cm broad; lower surface pitted, greenish brown; apothecia very common, the disc
epruinose; the spores 6-13 septate,
fusiform. Widespread on deciduous trees in open woods. This species is part of a difficult group
with expanded lobes and numerous apothecia. *Collema leucopeplum* Tuck. differs chiefly in having a white pruinose disc and is
most common in the southern
states. *C. subnigrescens* Degel.,
known from Florida, has 5-6 septate clavate spores.

12b Upper surface not pustulate but smooth to wrinkled; lobes
     usually crowded; thallus 3 cm or less in diameter. 13

13a Thallus 0.5-1.0 cm broad; apothecia dispersed. Fig. 233. ....
....Collema fragrans (Sm.) Ach.

Thallus dark olive green to brown
or black, closely adnate, 0.5-1.0 cm
broad; lobes more or less inflated, suberect; apothecia common, the spores
muriform. Widespread on deciduous
trees in open woods but easily overlooked because of the small size. Collema microptychium Tuck. also has a
tiny cushioned thallus but the spores
are needle-like and transversely many
septate.

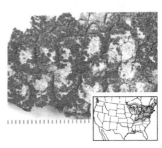

Figure 233.

13b Thallus 2-3 cm broad, pulvinate, apothecia abundant and
crowded. Fig. 234. ....Collema conglomeratum Hoffm.

Thallus dark brown, closely
adnate, 2-3 cm broad; lobes
narrow and crowded; lower
surface tan or buff, naked;
apothecia very abundant, the
spores 1-septate. Common on
deciduous trees in open woods
or along roadsides. C. cyrtaspis
Tuck. is probably equally common and differs only in having
3-septate spores. Microscopic
examination may also find C.
leptaleum Tuck., which is simi-
lar in habit but has long multiseptate spores, or C. callibotrys
Tuck., which has muriform spores.

Figure 234.

14a Thallus firmly attached, collected on limestone. Fig. 235. ....
.... Collema polycarpon Hoffm.

Thallus olive green to dark
brown, adnate, 2-5 cm broad;
lobes swollen with a raised margin; lower surface olive green;
apothecia numerous, the spores
1- or 2-septate. Widespread on
limestone outcrops. In the same
habitats one finds Leptogium
apalachense Nyl., which has 3-5
septate muriform spores. Other
confusable species include Collema multipartitum Sm., which

Figure 235.

has richly branched, less swollen, linear, convex lobes, and *C. cris-pum* (Huds.) Wigg., which has broader lobes and a rosettiform thallus.

14b Thallus adnate to loosely adnate, collected on soil or on mosses over soil or rocks (*Collema ryssoleum* also grows on acidic rocks). 15

15a Upper surface pustulate; thallus growing on acidic rocks. Fig. 236. ....*Collema ryssoleum* (Tuck.) Schneid.

Thallus olive or dark brown, adnate, 3-6 cm broad; lower surface olive greenish brown, smooth; apothecia very numerous, the spores 3-4 septate. Widespread on acidic rocks in eastern North America. This is the nonisidiate variant of *C. flaccidum.*

Figure 236.

15b Upper surface plane to deeply wrinkled; thallus growing on soil or over mosses on soil or rocks. 16

16a Thallus uniformly black to brownish black, the surface dull (under hand lens). Fig. 237. ....*Collema tenax* (Sw.) Ach.

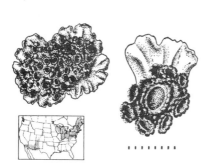

Thallus blackish brown, adnate, 3-6 cm broad; upper surface shiny, verrucose, the lobes irregular and crowded; apothecia common, the spores muriform, 20-25μ long. Widespread on soil in open areas. This is the most common soil *Collema* but is usually overlooked. A minor variant, *C. bachmanianum* (Fink) Degel., has a crenate apothecial rim and larger spores (30μ long). Other soil Collemas include *C. coccophorum* Tuck. with 1-septate spores and numerous erect lobules, and *C. limosum* (Ach.) Ach., which has a subcrustose thallus and 4 muriform spores per ascus rather than 8.

Figure 237.

16b Thallus slate blue, dark olive green, or dark brown, the surface shiny. 17

17a Lobes finely dissected and lobulate. Fig. 238. ....
....*Leptogium lichenoides* (**L.**) **Zahlbr.**

Thallus dark brown, often pulvinate, adnate, 4-8 cm broad; upper surface finely wrinkled; apothecia usually absent. Widespread in deep woods, often on rotting logs, but easily overlooked because the thallus blends with the substratum. *Leptogium californicum* Tuck., common in the western states, has less finely divided lobes and a smooth cortex.

Figure 238.

17b Lobes not finely dissected, dentate to smooth. 18

18a Lower surface with dense whitish tomentum. Fig. 239. ....
....*Leptogium inflexum* **Nyl.**

Thallus bluish mineral gray to brown, loosely adnate on mosses over rocks or on bark, 3-5 cm broad; upper surface plane to undulating; apothecia common, the rim finely lobulate, the spores muriform. Rare from southern Arizona and New Mexico into Mexico. The only other tomentose nonisidiate species that will be collected here is *L. rugosum* Sierk, which lacks lobules on the apothecia and has long 3-4 septate spores.

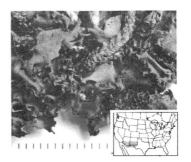

Figure 239.

18b Lower surface smooth, without tomentum (but with irregular tufts of hairs in *Leptogium platynum***).** 19

19a Upper surface smooth; eastern United States. Fig. 240. ....
....*Leptogium juniperinum* **Tuck.**

Thallus bluish to dark brown, adnate over mosses on soil or rocks, 3-6 cm broad; upper surface plane; apothecia common. Widespread in North America in sheltered areas but rather inconspicuous and rarely collected. It might be mistaken for *Collema tenax*, another gelatinous soil lichen, and they would have to be separated microscopically by proving a cortical layer in the *Leptogium* but none in the *Collema*.

Figure 240.

19b **Upper surface wrinkled (use hand lens); western North America. Fig. 241.** ....*Leptogium palmatum* (**Huds.**) **Mont.**

Figure 241.

Thallus bluish olive green to dark brown, loosely adnate on mosses on soil or over rocks, 5-8 cm broad; upper surface shiny, lobes becoming dissected, 100μ thick, slightly convoluted, suberect; lower surface dull, naked; apothecia common. Widespread over mosses in open areas. *Leptogium platynum* Herre, another western species, has a similar but much thicker thallus (more than 150μ). *L. sinuatum* (Huds.) Mass., chiefly western but occurring sporadically eastward, has a smaller thallus with flattened lobe tips.

III. Umbilicate Lichens

Most umbilicate lichens belong to the genus *Umbilicaria*, a small but conspicuous group known as the Rock Tripes. They are attached below by a single central cord (see Fig. 27). The main differences between species are presence or absence of rhizines, isidia, and presence of pustules. The group has been subdivided into several genera (*Actinogyra, Agyrophora, Omphalodiscus, Lasallia,* and *Umbilicaria*) on the basis of the convolutions of the apothecial disc (see Llano, 1950), but for the purposes of this book only one genus is used. Several other genera in the key mimic the umbilicate growth form and are included here. The commonest one is *Dermatocarpon miniatum*. All of the umbilicate lichens tend to be leathery and brittle and should be moistened before removing from the rock.

1a **Thallus yellowish green.** 2

1b **Thallus whitish mineral gray to blackish or brown.** 3

2a **Thallus 1-2 cm broad, closely adnate, the lobes often crowded. Fig. 242.** .... *Lecanora chrysoleuca* (**Sm.**) **Ach.**

Thallus greenish to olive yellow, umbilicate to lobate-crustose; lower surface tan to olive brown, naked; apothecia very common, flesh-colored. Cortex K+ more deeply yellow (usnic acid). Common on exposed rocks. The thalli, though scattered, may cover extensive areas of rock, and are easily plucked off with a knife.

Figure 242.

2b Thallus 3-8 cm broad, not closely attached. Fig. 243. ....
......................................Omphalodium arizonicum (Will.) Tuck.

Thallus dull yellowish green, leathery; upper surface ridged, coarsely papillate; lower surface ridged, black to dark brown, sparsely rhizinate, the rhizines coarse, flattened; apothecia very common. On exposed rocks and cliff faces. This very unusual lichen is known at higher elevations in Arizona, New Mexico, and Colorado. It intergrades with very large specimens of Lecanora chrysoleuca.

Figure 243.

3a Upper surface covered with fine short isidia (under hand lens). Fig. 244. ....Umbilicaria douota (L.) Baumg.

Thallus dark brown, 1-5 cm broad, fragile; upper surface plane; lower surface dark brown, naked; apothecia very rare. Medulla C+, KC+ red, (gyrophoric acid). On exposed boulders and cliffs. The thalli may be quite scattered and inconspicuous but the isidia make identification certain.

Figure 244.

3b Upper surface without isidia. 4

4a Lower surface more or less uniformly rhizinate or covered with flat plates. 5

4b Lower surface bare or finely papillate (under lens) (but in some Umbilicarias with sparse marginal rhizines). 11

5a Lower surface and rhizines black. 6

5b Lower surface and rhizines brown to pale tan or pink. 7

6a Thallus gray to whitish, usually pruinose. Fig. 245. ....
.... *Umbilicaria vellea* (L.) Ach.

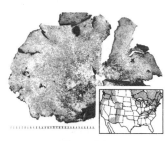

Figure 245.

Thallus 4-15 cm broad, leathery; upper surface scabrid or white pruinose; lower surface densely rhizinate, the rhizines coarse and simple; apothecia very rare. Medulla C+, KC+ red (gyrophoric acid). On exposed cliffs and boulders. A typical habitat for this relatively rare rock tripe is moist vertical cliffs. *U. mammulata* (below) intergrades with it but lacks pruina, has more delicate rhizines, and is brownish.

6b Thallus brown. Fig. 246. ....
.... *Umbilicaria mammulata* (Ach.) Tuck.

Figure 246.

Thallus 3-25 cm broad, leathery; upper surface plane; lower surface densely rhizinate, the rhizines branched; apothecia rare, the disc with concentric fissures. Medulla C+, KC+ red (gyrophoric acid). Very common on large boulders in open woods. This is by far the commonest *Umbilicaria* in eastern North America. A similar but more fragile and crowded plant, *U. caroliniana* Tuck., is found at high elevations in Tennessee and North Carolina.

From California northward to British Columbia one will find *U. polyrrhiza* (L.) Ach., a small brown species with radiate fissures on the apothecia. In the same habitats one may find *U. angulata* Tuck., which has a rimose upper surface. Another western species, *U. hirsuta* (Westr.) Ach., is unusual in having laminal soredia.

7a Lower surface with long, pointed, light brown or pink rhizines. Fig. 247. .... *Umbilicaria virginis* Schaer.

Thallus whitish mineral gray, 2-6 cm broad; upper surface lightly scabrid and pruinose; lower surface densely rhizinate; apothecia very common, the disc plane, with a central fissure. Medulla C+, KC+ red (gyrophoric acid). Common on large boulders in more sheltered areas. *U. cylindrica* (L.) Del. is very close in appearance of the lower surface but has discs with concentric fissures. Both are typical arctic species.

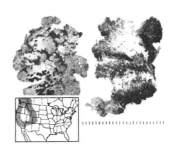

Figure 247.

7b Lower surface with short rhizines or with numerous flattened plates. **8**

8a Upper surface with black dots (perithecia) (use hand lens). Fig. 248. .... *Dermatocarpon moulinsii* (Mont.) **Zahlbr.**

Thallus whitish mineral gray, 2-6 cm broad; upper surface scabrid and white pruinose; lower surface brown, papillate and densely short rhizinate; perithecia abundant. On boulders in sheltered areas. Closely related *D. reticulatum* Magn. lacks distinct rhizines but is papillate.

Figure 248.

8b Upper surface without black dots **9**

9a Upper surface reticulately ridged toward the center (without lens). Fig. 249. .... *Umbilicaria proboscidea* (L.) **Schrad.**

Thallus blackish brown, 3-6 cm broad, fragile; upper surface whitish toward the center; lower surface mineral gray, sparsely rhizinate; apothecia common, the disc with concentric fissures. Medulla C+, KC+ red (gyrophoric acid). Common on exposed rocks and talus in boreal, alpine, or arctic regions. The edge of the thallus often has a white fringe of hyphae.

Figure 249.

9b Upper surface lacking ridges. **10**

10a Margin of thallus perforate and lacerated; rhizines sparse.
Fig. 250. ....*Umbilicaria torrefacta* (**Lightf.**) **Schrad.**

Thallus dark brown, 2-5 cm broad, fragile; upper surface smooth to wrinkled; lower surface light brown, the rhizines mostly flattened; apothecia common, the disc with concentric fissures. Medulla C+, KC+ red (gyrophoric acid). On exposed rocks in arctic-alpine localities.

Figure 250.

10b Margin of thallus irregular to entire; numerous plates below.
Fig. 251. ....*Umbilicaria muhlenbergii* (**Ach.**) **Tuck.**

Thallus light brown, 3-12 cm broad; upper surface plane to irregularly pitted; lower surface densely covered with plates; apothecia very common, sunken, the disc with radiating fissures. Medulla C+, KC+ red (gyrophoric acid). Common on exposed outcrops. *U. papulosa*, which often occurs with this species, may be separated by the regular raised pustules and bare lower surface.

Figure 251.

11a Upper surface with raised pustules (without hand lens). Fig.
252. ....*Umbilicaria papulosa* (**Ach.**) **Nyl.**

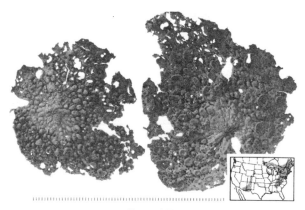

Figure 252.

Thallus light brown, sometimes turning dull red, 3-15 cm broad, fragile; upper surface becoming lacerated toward the edges; lower surface brown or tan, deeply pitted, naked; apothecia very common, black, the disc smooth. Medulla C+, KC+ red (gyrophoric acid). Very common on exposed rocks in large outcrops or cliffs and in open woods. *Umbilicaria pensylvanica* Hoffm. is identical from above but has a jet black lower surface. It grows with *U. papulosa* but is somewhat rarer. The European species *U. pustulata* (L.) Mér., which has cylindrical isidia, has been collected very rarely in upper New York.

11b Upper surface plane, undulating, or ridged. 12

12a Upper surface with numerous black dots (perithecia) (use hand lens). Fig. 253. .... *Dermatocarpon miniatum* (L.) Mann.

Thallus pale brown, 2-5 cm broad, plane or becoming convoluted and crowded; lower surface dusky, smooth. Widespread on limestone and sandstone outcrops. This is a very variable lichen that can be confused with Umbilicarias and especially with *D. fluviatile* (see p. 99). There is a great deal of variation in degree of crowding of the thallus, ranging from simple orbicular thalli to convoluted and crowded colonies. In the western states it occurs with *D. reticulatum* Magn., which differs in having a strongly papillate lower surface.

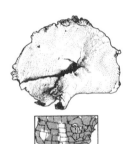

Figure 253.

12b Upper surface without dots (black apothecial discs and pycnidia may be present). 13

13a Upper surface conspicuously reticulate, especially toward the center, the ridges whitish granular. Fig. 254. ....
...................................*Umbilicaria krascheninnikovii* (Sav.) Zahlbr.

Thallus dark mineral gray, 2-3 cm broad; lower surface more or less uniformly brown, naked; apothecia common, the disc centrally fissured. Common on exposed boulders and cliffs. *Umbilicaria decussatus* (Vill.) Zahlbr., a rare alpine species, is very similar but has a black or mottled lower surface and larger thallus.

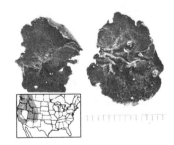

Figure 254.

13b **Upper surface without conspicuous reticulate ridges.** 14
14a **Upper surface finely reticulately rugose (use lens). Fig. 255.**
.... *Umbilicaria hyperborea* (**Ach.**) **Ach.**

Figure 255.

Thallus dark brown, 2-5 cm broad; lower surface dark brown, naked, pitted; apothecia common, the disc with concentric fissures. Medulla C+, KC+ red (gyrophoric acid). Widespread on exposed rocks in alpine or arctic regions. *Umbilicaria polyphylla* (.L.) Baumg. is much rarer and distinguished by crowded or grouped thalli.

14b **Upper surface smooth and continuous. Fig. 256.** ....
.... *Umbilicaria phaea* **Tuck.**

Figure 256.

Thallus brown, 2-3 cm broad; lower surface smooth to finely papillate, brown; apothecia very common, the disc concentrically fissured. Medulla C+, KC+ red, (gyrophoric acid). Very common on boulders and cliffs in open areas from southern California to British Columbia, rarer from New Mexico to Montana. This appears to be the commonest *Umbilicaria* on the West Coast.

IV. Fruticose Lichens

Fruticose lichens form a very large group of unrelated species that share a shrubby, hairlike, or strap-shaped growth form. The typical thallus consists of a main branch with or without numerous side branches. In *Cladonia* the branches are hollow but in other genera the medulla is more or less filled with hyphae. A number of different families fall together in neat packages, such as the Cladoniaceae, Stereocaulaceae, and Usneaceae and the genera can be recognized at sight rather easily. Once one learns the genera, keying can be speeded up by going directly to the common genera as follows:

The genus *Cladonia* is by far the most widespread fruticose lichen and will be collected very frequently, even in cities. A specialized terminology has built up around *Cladonia*. For example, the small scale-like squamules, crowded into mats, form the primary thallus (Fig. 257D). When only these squamules are present, it is very difficult to identify them to species (see Key V on p. 203). One should avoid collecting sterile squamules. Fertile squamules will be recognized because they bear erect, simple or branched structures called podetia (Fig. 257) (singular podetium) on which in turn brown or red apothecia are borne. These podetia differ in shape, color, openings in the axils (Fig. 257B), and presence of soredia. Most Cladonias have a primary thallus that persists, as well as erect podetia, but the reindeer mosses (*Cladonia rangiferina* and relatives) lack primary squamules and have highly developed, branched podetia.

Thomson (1967) has written a technical summary of *Cladonia* in North America which can be consulted by advanced students. Chemistry plays a very important role in this genus and this aspect is discussed in detail by Thomson.

1a Thallus hollow (section with razor blade) and always round in cross section, usually brittle when dry; squamules often present. *Cladonia, Dactylina,* and *Thamnolia.* 2

1b Thallus solid, usually not brittle, round or flat in cross section; squamules lacking. 73

2a Podetia (see Fig. 257) growing free on soil or among mosses; squamules always lacking. 3

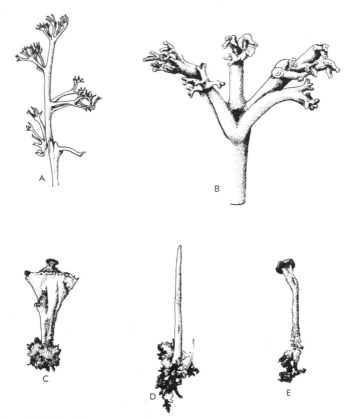

Figure 257. *Cladonia* structures. A, finely branched podetium without squamules;
B, open axil; C, cup shaped; D, pointed and sterile; E, pointed and fertile.

2b Podetia more or less attached to soil, bark, or rock; squamules
always present on podetia or at the base of podetia. 17

3a Podetia finely branched (without lens) (Fig. 257A), the outer
cortex lacking and the surface dull and fibrous (use hand
lens). 4

3b Podetia simple and unbranched to moderately branched; cortex
present, the surface smooth and shiny. 8

4a Colonies forming discrete compacted heads; distinct main
branches lacking. Fig. 258. ....*Cladonia alpestris* (L.) Rabenh.

Figure 258.

Podetia pale yellowish gray, 6-10 cm high, the colonies separate or loosely clumped; pycnidia common, apothecia very rare. On soil and mossy humus in open woods or pastures. This unmistakable species is rare in the southern part of its range. From North Carolina to Texas a very similar species, *C. evansii* Abb., grows on sterile white sand; it is ashy white and lacks usnic acid but contains atranorin and perlatolic acid. Both of these species are frequently collected for use as imitation shrubbery and trees in model train layouts.

4b Colonies forming scattered entangled masses without discrete heads; distinct main branches usually present. 5

5a Podetia whitish ashy gray; surface K+ yellow. Fig. 259. Reindeer Moss. ....*Cladonia rangiferina* (L.) Wigg.

Podetia 6-10 cm high, the colonies often extensive; branching pattern mostly in fours, the axils open; pycnidia common, apothecia very rare, dark brown. K+ yellow (atranorin), P+ red (fumarprotocetraric acid). Common on soil and humus in open areas. This well-known lichen will usually occur with yellowish species as *C. subtenuis* and *C. arbuscula* and by holding up the species together in bright light or sunshine, the ashy gray color can be distinguished from the pale yellowish gray of the other two.

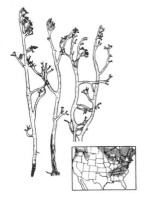

Figure 259.

5b Podetia yellowish or greenish gray (usnic acid); surface K— or brownish. 6

6a Axils of branches closed (use hand lens); tips mostly in pairs. Fig. 260. .... *Cladonia subtenuis* (**Abb.**) **Evans**

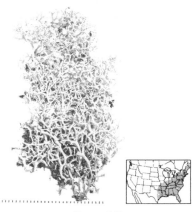

Podetia 4-8 cm tall, often forming mats up to a foot in diameter; pycnidia common, apothecia very rare. P+ red (fumarprotocetraric acid). Common on sandy soil in open pine forests and along roadsides. This is undoubtedly the most frequently collected "Reindeer Moss" in southeastern United States, often growing with *C. rangiferina*. In mountainous areas and the northern part of its range it may occur with *C. arbuscula* or *C. mitis*, from which it must be carefully dis-

Figure 260.

tinguished by branching pattern, axils, and chemical tests. In the Pacific Northwest one may collect *C. tenuis* (Flk.) Harm., a very closely related species with more distinct main stems.

6b Axils of branches open (see Fig. 257B) (use hand lens); tips in 3's and 4's. 7

7a Tips of branches P+ red; ultimate branches rather coarse, strongly pointing in one direction. Fig. 261. .... *Cladonia arbuscula* (**Wallr.**) **Rabenh.**

Podetia 6-10 cm tall, the colonies often extensive, the ultimate branches mostly pointing in one direction; pycnidia common, apothecia very rare, dark brown. P+ red (fumarprotocetraric acid). Common on soil and humus in open pastures and fields. Without a P test, this species is difficult to separate from *C. mitis*, which generally has ultimate branches pointing in various directions.

Figure 261.

7b Tips of branches P—; ultimate branches finer, not strongly oriented in one direction. Fig. 262. ....*Cladonia mitis* **Sandst.**

Podetia 4-8 cm tall, forming extensive colonies; branches generally in threes, rarely fours; pycnidia common. Widespread in open pine forests and along roadsides. The P test is essential to distinguish this species from the much more common *C. subtenuis* group. There are several other P— species, all mostly arctic or boreal but extending into New England and the Great Lakes region: *C. impexa* Harm., which has perlatolic acid; *C. submitis* Evans, which has robust coarse main steams and branches in fours; and *C. terrae-novae* Ahti, which is K+ yellow (atranorin).

Figure 262.

8a Apothecia and pycnidia red (use hand lens), K+ purple. Fig. 263. ....*Cladonia leporina* **Fr.**
Podetia yellowish green, leathery, prostrate, 3-6 cm high, forming mats 5-10 cm broad; pycnidia and apothecia common, dark red. P+ yellow (baeomycic acid). Common on sandy soil and stumps in open areas. This is frequently collected and can be recognized at sight. *C. caroliniana* has a similar aspect but differs in being very brittle and lacking red apothecia.

Figure 263.

8b Apothecia and pycnidia (if present) brown, K—. 9

9a Squamules present on branches (use hand lens). ....
............*Cladonia furcata* (see p. 165)

9b Squamules completely lacking. 10

10a Podetia light greenish yellow, usually much branched. 11

10b Thallus white or brownish, simple or little branched. 16

11a Tips of podetia flaring into shallow cups. Fig. 264. ....
....*Cladonia amaurocraea* (Flk.) Schaer.

Podetia 6-10 cm tall, erect, very brittle when dry, completely corticate and shiny, sparingly branched, the axils open, expanding into proliferating cups; pycnidia common but apothecia rare. On soil and humus over rocks in open areas. In the southern part of its range, this species becomes quite rare but can be confused with *C. uncialis,* which lacks true cups and has shorter blunter tips.

Figure 264.

11b Tips pointed, not cup-forming. 12
12a Podetia coarse, with large perforations. Fig. 265. ....
....*Cladonia boryi* Tuck.

Podetia light yellowish green, 4-8 cm tall, sparingly branched, the surface pitted; pycnidia common, apothecia very rare, dark brown. On soil and humus in open areas, especially near large outcrops. This species is rare in the southern part of its range but can easily be recognized by the coarse pitted podetia. *C. perforata* Evans, known from 3 localities in Florida, also has perforations but the cortex is smooth.

Figure 265.

12b Podetia generally thinner (except in some forms of *Cladonia uncialis*), perforations lacking or very tiny. 13
13a Surface of podetia dull, covered with fine hairs at the tip (use high power lens). Fig. 266. ....*Cladonia pachycladodes* Vain.

Podetia pale greenish yellow, prostrate, 1-2 cm tall, forming mats 5-10 cm broad; cortex covered with a fine tomentum composed of loose hyphae; pycnidia and apothecia very rare. Widespread on barren sandy soil in the Coastal Plain. Though similar to *C. caroliniana* in having irregularly thickened podetia, this *Cladonia* can be recognized immediately by the peculiar dull cortex.

Figure 266. A, branch tip (X10).

13b Surface of podetia shiny, without hairs. 14

14a Podetia very fine, hair-like, 0.3-0.6 mm in diameter. Fig. 267.
....*Cladonia subsetacea* **Evans**

Podetia light greenish yellow, prostrate, 1-2 cm tall, forming mats 4-8 cm broad; pycnidia and apothecia very rare. P+ yellow (in Florida specimens P−) (squamatic acid with or without baeomycic acid). Widespread on open sandy soil in the Coastal Plain from North Carolina to Florida. Hair-like fine podetial branches characterize this rather rare *Cladonia*. Some forms of *C. caroliniana* might appear similar but the branches are at least 1 mm wide.

Figure 267.

14b Podetia thicker, 1 mm or more in diameter. 15

15a Side branches usually well developed; podetia generally thin, 1-2 mm in diameter. Fig. 268. ......*Cladonia uncialis* **(L.) Wigg.**

Podetia yellowish green, usually more or less prostrate, 3-6 cm tall, brittle, richly branched, corticate and appearing speckled green under a lens; pycnidia common, apothecia rare, dark brown. On soil and humus, especially over rocks, in pastures, rocky slopes, and other open areas. It is very similar to *C. amaurocraea* but never forms cups. There is very troublesome intergradation with *C. caroliniana* in the southern part of its range and some specimens cannot be positively identified as either species.

Figure 268.

15b Side branches not as numerous, generally short; podetia often very thick, 3-6 mm in diameter. Fig. 269. ....
................................*Cladonia caroliniana* (**Schwein.**) **Tuck.**

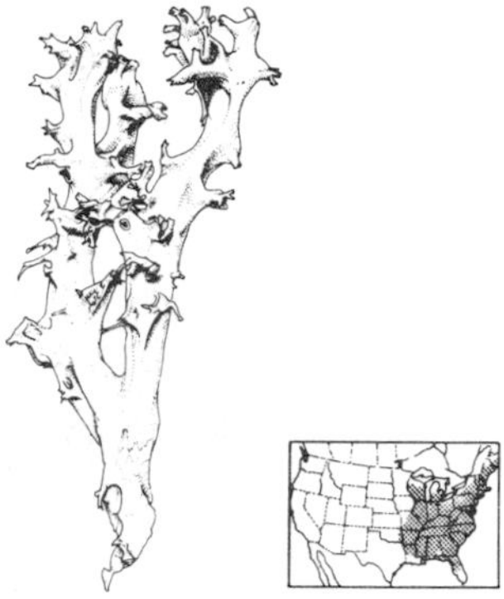

Figure 269.

Podetia greenish yellow, brittle, erect to prostrate, 3-6 cm high, irregularly inflated, and lacerated, smooth or with bristle-like secondary branches; pycnidia common, apothecia rare, dark brown. Common on sandy soil and humus in open areas. In the typical irregularly inflated form this species is unmistakable, growing in large mats along the edges of large rock outcrops, but forms with narrow podetia intergrade with *C. uncialis* to such an extent that the two species can hardly be distinguished.

16a Thallus white, pointed and worm-like. Fig. 270. ....
................................*Thamnolia subuliformis* (**Ehrh.**) **Culb.**

Figure 270.

Thallus 3-6 cm long, with some side branches, erect or prostrate; pycnidia and apothecia unknown. K+ yellowish, P+ yellow (baeomycic acid). Very common on exposed soil and among mosses. There is hardly a place in the Arctic where one will not find the scattered thalli of this unique lichen. A chemical variant, *T. vermicularis* (Sw.) Schaer., makes up one-third to one-half of the specimens collected; it is K+ deep yellow (thamnolic acid).

16b Thallus brownish, inflated, blunt, finger-like. Fig. 271. ....
................................*Dactylina arctica* (**Hook.**) **Nyl.**

Figure 271.

Thallus 2-4 cm tall, scattered or growing in mats 4-8 cm broad; apothecia unknown. P+ red (unknowns). Common on soil and among mosses in arctic Canada and southward into Oregon and Washington. This is one of the best known arctic lichens. *Dactylina madreporiformis*

(Ach.) Tuck. is a smaller stubby plant common at high elevations in the Rockies; it is P—. A pruinose species, *D. ramulosa* (Hook.) Tuck., occurs in the arctic and as far south as Montana.

17a Podetia forming distinct cups (see Fig. 257C). 18

17b Podetia not cup-shaped but forming pointed or blunt clubs (see Fig. 257D), often tipped with apothecia (see Fig. 257E) (if branched, irregular cups may be formed by the expanded axils). 35

18a Apothecia (or if sterile pycnidia) bright red (use hand lens for pycnidia), K+ purple. 19

18b Apothecia and pycnidia pale to dark brown, K— or K+ brownish; or apothecia and pycnidia lacking. 22

19a Podetia smooth, without any soredia. Fig. 272. ....
....*Cladonia coccifera* (L.) Willd.

Cups yellowish green, stout, 1-2 cm tall, sometimes proliferating marginally, the surface covered with scattered areoles; primary squamules well developed at the base of podetia; pycnidia and apothecia very common. Widespread on soil and on humus over rocks in open alpine or arctic areas. Closely related *C. pleurota* has distinct granular soredia.

Figure 272.

19b Podetia covered with powdery soredia. 20

20a Podetia whitish gray, the surface K+ deep yellow. Fig. 273.
....*Cladonia digitata* (L.) Hoffm.

Cups whitish to yellowish mineral gray, 1.5-4.0 cm high, rarely proliferating marginally, corticate toward the base but becoming densely sorediate toward the upper part; primary squamules large, sorediate; apothecia and pycnidia common, blood red. K+, P+ deep yellow (thamnolic acid). Rare on humus and over mosses in open areas or swamps.

Figure 273.

20b Podetia yellow to greenish yellow, the surface K— or turning yellowish green. **21**

21a Cups short and stout. Fig. 274. ....
....*Cladonia pleurota* (**Flk.**) **Schaer.**

Figure 274.

Cups stout, 1-2 cm tall, rarely proliferating, sorediate in the upper parts and inside the cup; primary squamules distinct, medium-sized; pycnidia and apothecia common, deep red. Common on soil and on humus over rocks in the open. At first this distinctive cup *Cladonia* will be confused with greenish forms of the *C. chlorophaea* group until the red pycnidia are seen. *C. deformis* has much taller, narrow cups.

21b Cups tall and narrow. Fig. 275. ....
....*Cladonia deformis* (**L.**) **Hoffm.**

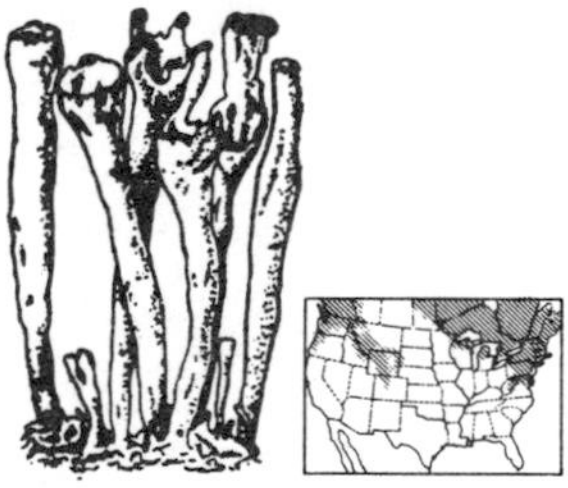

Figure 275.

Cups yellowish green, 2-4 cm tall, irregularly expanded, diffusely sorediate but with corticate areas near the base; primary squamules medium-sized, sparsely developed; pycnidia common, apothecia rather rare, blood red. Widespread on humus and rotting logs in swamps and open areas. Generally only a few podetia will be found at a time. *C. gonecha* (Ach.) Asah. is virtually indistinguishable except for larger primary squamules (5-10 mm long) and the presence of squamatic acid with or without bellidiflorin. Both of these have much taller, narrower cups than *C. pleurota*.

22a Podetia covered with powdery or granular soredia. **23**

22b Podetia lacking soredia (*Cladonia pyxidata* has **coarse areoles** and *C. squamosa* fine dense squamules). **28**

23a Cups deep, stout to elongate, distinct. **24**

23b Cups shallow, poorly developed, podetia in part pointed or lacerated at the tips. **27**

24a Cups yellow (usnic acid present). Fig. 276. ....
....*Cladonia carneola* (Fr.) Fr.

Cups 1.5-3.0 cm high, sometimes proliferating marginally, diffusely sorediate; primary squamules small, incised, poorly developed; pycnidia common, apothecia rather rare, pale brown. Rare on humus and soil in open areas. It resembles *C. chlorophaea* but has a distinctive yellowish cast and more extensive powdery soredia. The brown pycnidia and apothecia will separate it from red-fruited *C. pleurota*.

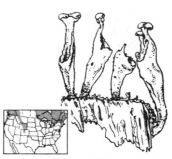

Figure 276.

24b Cups greenish gray to faint brownish. 25

25a Soredia coarse and granular; cups generally stout. Fig. 277.
....*Cladonia chlorophaea* (Flk.) Spreng.

Cups 0.5-1.5 cm high, greenish mineral gray, simple or proliferating marginally, the axils closed; soredia granular, quite diffuse to sparse, intergrading with areoles; primary squamules rather coarse, sparsely to moderately developed; apothecia rare, dark brown. Widespread and common on soil and over mosses on roadbanks, over rocks, and at bases of trees. This is the most commonly collected cup *Cladonia*. There are four chemical populations which can only be separated by microchemical crystal tests: *C. chlorophaea* (fumarprotocetraric acid), *C. grayi* Merr. (grayanic with or without fumarprotocetraric), *C. cryptochlorophaea* Asah. (cryptochlorophaeic with or without fumarprotocetraric), and *C. merochlorophaea* Asah. (merochlorophaeic with or without fumarprotocetraric). *C. merochlorophaea* has the most restricted range, Connecticut to Minnesota, while *C. grayi* and *C. cryptochlorophaea* occur throughout eastern North America.

Figure 277.

25b Soredia fine and powdery; cups generally thinner. 26

26a Cups deep and expanded. Fig. 278. ....
.... *Cladonia conista* (**Ach.**) **Robb.**

Figure 278.

Cups whitish mineral gray, 0.5-1.0 cm tall; soredia farinose, diffuse; primary squamules coarse, numerous; apothecia very rare. P+ red (fumarprotocetraric acid) or P−. Widespread on soil and over mosses in open areas. *C. major* (Hag.) Sandst. is very similar except for being about twice as large and lacking substance H. Both intergrade with and must be carefully distinguished from *C. chlorophaea*.

26b Cups tall, not expanded. Fig. 279. ....
....*Cladonia fimbriata* (**L.**) **Fr.**

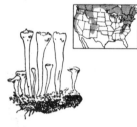

Figure 279.

Cups whitish mineral gray, narrow, 1-3 cm high, rarely proliferating marginally; soredia farinose, diffuse; primary squamules small, sparsely developed; apothecia rare, dark brown. P+ red (fumarprotocetraric acid). Widespread on soil in open areas. This species intergrades with both *C. conista* and *C. chlorophaea* but is generally recognized by the narrower cups.

27a Cups lacerated at the tips, the margins rolled inward. Fig. 280. ....*Cladonia cenotea* (**Ach.**) **Schaer.**

Figure 280.

Podetia whitish mineral gray, 1-3 cm tall, narrow, sparingly branched in the upper parts; becoming squamulate toward the base, soredia diffuse over most of the surface; primary squamules medium-sized; pycnidia common, apothecia rare, dark brown. Widespread on rotten stumps and wood and on soil or humus in open areas. The asymmetrical cups with margins rolled inward are characteristic of this northern *Cladonia*.

27b Cups entire, often very small, the margins flaring. Fig. 281.
....*Cladonia nemoxyna* (**Ach.**) **Nyl.**

Podetia whitish mineral gray, 1.0-2.5
cm tall, simple or sparingly branched,
pointed or flaring into small irregular
cups, the rim becoming indented or
proliferating, sparsely sorediate over
most of the surface but with bare ecorticate areas usually showing, squamulate
toward the base; primary squamules
tiny; pycnidia common. P+ (fumarprotocetraric acid) or P−. Rare on soil and
humus in pastures or on roadbanks. This

Figure 281.

difficult and variable species will probably be confused with *C.
fimbriata* if the cups are well developed or with species like *C.
decorticata* if cups are lacking.

28a Cups proliferating from the centers. Fig. 282. ....
....*Cladonia verticillata* (**Hoffm.**) **Schaer.**

Podetia greenish mineral gray, 2-8
cm tall, smooth to moderately squamulate; primary squamules small, generally poorly developed; pycnidia and
apothecia common, dark brown. P+
red (fumarprotocetraric acid). Widespread on soil in pastures and along
roadsides. This species can be recognized at sight by the unusual verticil-
late cups. Toward the southern part of
its range it occurs intermingled with
C. calycantha Nyl., which is chemically
the same but has flatter abruptly flar-

Figure 282.

ing cups and is free of squamules. In Florida one will find *C. rappii*
Evans, differentiated by the presence of psoromic acid (P+ yellow).

**28b Cups proliferating from the margins or not proliferating at
all.** **29**

29a Cups coarse and stout, usually not proliferating, covered with greenish areoles (see Fig. 257C). Fig. 283. ....
....*Cladonia pyxidata* (L.) **Hoffm.**

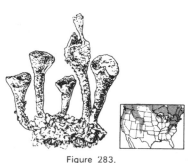

Figure 283.

Cups greenish mineral gray, 1.0-1.5 cm high, the surface very coarsely areolate and granular but not forming soredia; primary squamules often well developed, large; pycnidia common, apothecia rare, dark brown. P+ red (fumarprotocetraric acid). Common on humus and soil over rocks in open areas. When well developed, this is an easily recognized lichen but it intergrades with the *C. chlorophaea* group in the southern part of its range. The differences between small areoles and large granular soredia are often difficult to detect and one cannot avoid collecting specimens that seem to be intermediates.

29b Cups more attenuated, more or less proliferating, areoles not conspicuously developed. 30

30a Centers of cups closed (use hand lens). 31

30b Centers of cups open or perforated. 32

31a Cortex at tips of podetia shiny (use hand lens), continuous at the base. Fig. 284. ....*Cladonia gracilis* (L.) **Willd.**

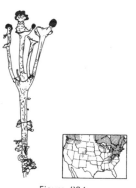

Figure 284.

Podetia brownish mineral gray, 2-8 cm tall. sparingly branched, the cups quite distinct to abortive, smooth to moderately squamulate; primary squamules generally poorly developed, often evanescent in the boreal forests; pycnidia and apothecia common, dark brown. P+ red (fumarprotocetraric acid). Common and widespread on soil, humus, and mosses in open areas. Probably no other *Cladonia* exhibits as much variation as this species, and there is not space to enumerate all of the varieties here. Basically it is recognized by the brownish tinge, marginally proliferating cups, and continuous shiny cortex.

31b Cortex at tips of podetia dull, and fibrous, the base black-spotted in older parts. Fig. 285. ....
....*Cladonia phyllophora* **(Ehrh.) Hoffm.**

Podetia whitish mineral gray, 3-5 cm tall, sparingly branched, the cups irregularly lacerate and partially obscured by squamules; primary squamules medium-sized, well developed; pycnidia and apothecia common, dark brown. P+ red (fumarprotocetraric acid). Rather rare on soil and over mosses in open areas. This species in its typical form is not usually confusable with other Cladonias that have squamulate irregularly cup-forming podetia. However, it must be carefully distinguished from *C. crispata* (K−) and *C. multiformis* (cups regularly perforate).

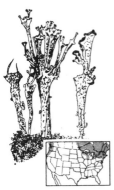

Figure 285.

32a Membrane of cups perforated with many small holes (use hand lens). Fig. 286. ....*Cladonia multiformis* **Mcrr.**

Podetia greenish to brownish mineral gray, 3-5 cm tall, sparsely to moderately squamulate, the cups proliferating marginally; primary squamules medium-sized, often sparsely developed; pycnidia very common, apothecia rare, dark brown. P+ red (fumarprotocetraric acid). Widespread on soil along road cuts and in open fields. This species is extremely variable in development of cups and density of squamules, but the perforate membrane is usually sufficiently distinct for positive identification. *C. crispata* (P−, squamatic acid) and *C. caraccensis* Vain. (K+ yellow thamnolic acid) are closely allied, rarer species best distinguished by the chemical features.

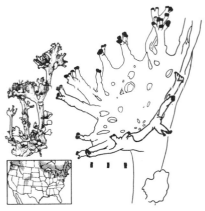

Figure 286.

32b Cups open and gaping. 33

33a **Podetia finely and densely squamulose (use hand lens). Fig. 287.** ....*Cladonia squamosa* (Scop.) **Hoffm.**

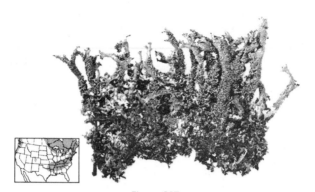

Figure 287.

Podetia greenish mineral gray, 3-6 cm tall, sparingly branched, forming irregular narrow cups, the axils open; primary squamules poorly developed or evanescent; pycnidia common, apothecia very rare. Widespread on soil and over mosses on rocks in mature forests. This common *Cladonia* may be difficult to identify at first because of the variability in cup development. It fluoresces brilliant white in UV. In the Pacific Northwest there is one chemical variant, *C. subsquamosa* (Nyl.) Vain. which is K+, P+ yellow (thamnolic acid).

33b **Podetia sparsely to moderately squamulose** 34
34a **Basal squamules large, 2-3 mm long. Fig. 288.** ....
...................................*Cladonia mateocyatha* **Robb.**

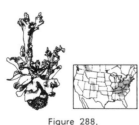

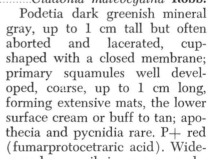

Figure 288.

Podetia dark greenish mineral gray, up to 1 cm tall but often aborted and lacerated, cup-shaped with a closed membrane; primary squamules well developed, coarse, up to 1 cm long, forming extensive mats, the lower surface cream or buff to tan; apothecia and pycnidia rare. P+ red (fumarprotocetraric acid). Widespread on soil in open woods, road cuts and soil banks. It often occurs with *C. apodocarpa,* which has more linear squamules with a chalky white lower surface. *C. turgida* is generally much larger and reacts K+ yellow (atranorin).

34b Basal squamules small or lacking. Fig. 289. ....
.... *Cladonia crispata* (**Ach.**) **Flot.**

Podetia brownish mineral gray, 5-8 cm tall, shiny, branched with flaring cups, the cups proliferating marginally, the axils open, sparsely to moderately squamulose; primary squamules evanescent; apothecia and pycnidia common, small, dark brown. K—, P— (squamatic acid). On soil or over mosses in open areas. Two chemical variants are restricted to the southeastern states: *C. atlantica* Evans which contains squamatic and baeomycic acids (P+ yellow) and *C. floridana* Evans which contains thamnolic acid (K+ yellow).

Figure 289.

35a Apothecia (if present) and pycnidia red (use hand lens), K+ purple. 36

35b Apothecia (if present) and pycnidia brown or black; or apothecia and pycnidia lacking. 43

36a Podetia and squamules lacking soredia. Fig. 290. British Soldiers. ....*Cladonia cristatella* **Tuck.**

Podetia yellowish green, 1-2 cm tall, branched toward the upper parts, smooth to moderately squamulate; primary squamules inconspicuous; apothecia and pycnidia very common. Very common on humus, soil, and rotting logs in open areas. This is one of the first lichens collected by a lichen student. In Florida it is replaced by *C. abbreviatula* Merr., a smaller species that reacts K+ yellow (didymic and thamnolic acids). In the Pacific Northwest and arctic Canada the common esorediate red-fruited species is *C. bellidiflora* (Ach.) Schaer., larger and more richly squamulate than *C. cristatella*.

Figure 290.

36b Podetia and/or squamules more or less covered with powdery soredia. 37

37a Podetia pale yellow (usnic acid present); Pacific Northwest. Fig. 291. ....*Cladonia transcendens* (Vain.) Vain.

Figure 291.

Podetia pale yellowish green to gray, 3-4 cm tall, sparsely to densely squamulate, sparingly branched and sometimes with narrow cups, the axils closed, sorediate toward the upper parts; primary squamules medium-sized to large, incised; pycnidia and apothecia common, red. K+, P+ yellow (thamnolic acid with or rarely without usnic acid). Widespread on stumps and decaying logs in open conifer forests. This is a western species separated from *C. bellidiflora* by the presence of soredia.

37b Podetia whitish to greenish mineral gray (usnic acid lacking except in *Cladonia incrassata*); eastern North America (*Cladonia bacillaris* and *C. macilenta* rarely in the west). 38

38a Surface of podetia instantly K+ deep yellow (thamnolic acid present). 39

38b Surface of podetia K− or slowly dingy yellow or brown. 40

39a Lower surface of squamules uniformly white. Fig. 292. ....
....*Cladonia macilenta* Hoffm.

Figure 292.

Podetia whitish mineral gray to white, 0.5-1.5 cm tall, unbranched to sparingly branched toward the apex; soredia farinose, diffuse; primary squamules sparse to dense, small; pycnidia common, apothecia rare, K+, P+ deep yellow orange (thamnolic acid). Common on fenceposts, shingles, and base of trees in the open. *C. bacillaris*, a more widespread species, differs only in chemistry (K−, P−). In the Coastal Plain from North Carolina through Florida to Texas one will find *C. ravenelii* Tuck., which has smaller podetia with many primary squamules and also reacts K+ yellow.

39b Lower surface of squamules with pale orange veins. Fig. 293.
....*Cladonia hypoxantha* **Tuck.**

Podetia whitish mineral gray, short and often poorly developed, 0.5-1.0 cm high, sorediate in the upper parts, inner cartilaginous layer pale orange; primary squamules well developed and forming extensive mats, sorediate, incised; pycnidia and apothecia rare, red. K+, P+ yellow (thamnolic acid). Widespread on humus and on rotting logs in open woods in Florida. Though at first appearing to be an indeterminate mass of squamules, this species is immediately recognized by the unique orange veins on the lower surface of the squamules.

Figure 293.

40a Primary squamules rather large (2-4 mm), sorediate. Fig. 294.
....*Cladonia incrassata* **Flk.**

Podetia greenish or yellowish mineral gray, 0.5-2.0 cm tall, smooth to sparsely squamulate; primary squamules becoming quite large and forming an extensive mat, powdery sorediate along the margins; apothecia common. On logs and base of trees in open woods or in swamps. *C. cristatella* is closely related but lacks any trace of soredia on the squamules.

Figure 294.

40b Primary squamules small and usually poorly developed; soredia sparse or lacking. **41**

41a Podetia commonly more or less branched, robust; large corticate areas remaining. Fig. 295. ....
....*Cladonia floerkeana* **(Fr.) Somm.**

Podetia whitish mineral gray, 0.5-2.5 cm tall, unbranched, smooth or covered with small squamules, sparsely to moderately sorediate but with distinct corticate areas toward the apex; primary squamules sparse, tiny, turning sorediate; apothecia common. Widespread on soil, logs, and humus in open areas. This species may be confused with *C. cristatella*, a much more common lichen which lacks any soredia. *C. bacillaris* and *C. macilenta* have extensive diffuse soredia and usually lack apothecia.

Figure 295.

41b Podetia usually simple, often pointed, largely ecorticate. 42

42a Ecorticate areas bare and darkening. Fig. 296. ....
....*Cladonia didyma* (Fée) Vain.

Podetia whitish mineral gray, 0.5-1.5 cm tall, mostly unbranched, sparsely to densely covered with granular or isidioid squamules, the ecorticate areas turning brownish and translucent; primary squamules usually dense, finely incised; apothecia common. Widespread on soil in open areas. This is probably the most common red-fruited *Cladonia* in the southeastern states. *C. bacillaris* is close but has farinose soredia and is usually larger.

Figure 296. (X2).

42b Ecorticate areas sorediate. Fig. 297. ....
....*Cladonia bacillaris* (Ach.) Nyl.

Podetia whitish mineral gray to white, 0.5-1.5 cm tall, unbranched to sparingly branched toward the apex, a few squamules developed at the base; soredia farinose, diffuse; primary squamules poorly developed to dense, small; pycnidia common, apothecia rare. K+ yellowish, P− or P+ yellowish (barbatic acid, rarely also didymic and usnic acids). Very common on fenceposts, shingles, and the base of trees in open areas throughout North America. *C. macilenta* differs only in chemistry (K+ deep yellow).

Figure 297. (X2).

43a Surface of podetia sorediate (use lens). 44

43b Surface of podetia without soredia (or podetia finely squamulose or lacking). 53

44a Podetia generally unbranched, 1-2 cm tall or less. 45

44b Podetia long and slender, usually branched several times (sometimes unbranched in *Cladonia cornuta*), 3-8 cm tall. 50

45a Podetia very short (1-3 mm), tipped with brown apothecia.
Fig. 298. ....*Cladonia parasitica* **(Hoffm.) Hoffm.**

Podetia greenish mineral gray, covered with fine isidioid squamules; primary squamules finely incised, forming
a dense mat, the margins becoming
isidioid; apothecia common. K+, P+
deep yellow (thamnolic acid). Common on rotten logs and stumps in deep
woods. A typical habitat is the cut surface of old stumps and it is difficult to
cut across the grain to get good specimens. *C. caespiticia* differs in chemistry
(K−) and less divided squamules. *C.*
botrytes is also K− but has pale flesh
colored apothecia.

Figure 298.

45b Podetia more than 5 mm tall, apothecia rare. 46

46a Primary squamules conspicuous (2-5 mm long), usually dark
green, podetia arising from the centers. Fig. 299. ....
........................*Cladonia coniocraea* **(Flk.) Spreng.**

Podetia whitish green, 0.5-2.0 cm tall, pointed
or forming narrow irregular cups, the soredia
farinose, corticate areas restricted to the base;
pycnidia common, apothecia rare, dark brown. P+
red (fumarprotocetraric acid). Common on humus and rotting logs in closed woods. This is
probably the most frequently collected pointed
Cladonia without apothecia. *C. ochrochlora* Flk. is
virtually identical except for larger esorediate
corticate areas, amounting to one-third or more
of the podetial surface. *C. incrassata* (see p. 159)
is similar and may key here. Check carefully for
red pycnidia. A rarer species in the western states,
C. bacilliformis (Nyl.) Vain., has identical morphology but is yellow (usnic and barbatic acids).

Figure 299.

46b Primary squamules small, less than 2 mm long, sometimes
finely divided, greenish mineral gray. 47

47a Podetia blunt, the base with coarse isidioid granules. Fig. 300.
....*Cladonia cylindrica* (Evans) **Evans**

Figure 300. (X2).

Podetia ashy white, 0.5-1.5 cm high, rarely branched, the tips blunt or slightly expanded into tiny shallow cups, diffusely sorediate, sparsely squamulate toward the base; primary squamules small, incised, usually well developed; pycnidia common, apothecia rare, dark brown. P+ red (fumarprotocetraric and grayanic acid). Very common on stumps, base of trees, rotten logs, and humus in open woods and pastures. Podetia are often only poorly developed. *C. coniocraea* is very similar but in general its squamules are much larger and greener with grayanic acid lacking. *C. balfourii* has more pointed podetia and also lacks grayanic acid.

47b Podetia pointed or tipped with apothecia. 48

48a Soredia powdery, more or less continuous over the podetial surface; southern United States. Fig. 301. ....
....*Cladonia balfourii* **Cromb.**

Figure 301.

Podetia ashy white, 1-2 cm tall, rarely branched, pointed or forming tiny cups, more or less diffusely sorediate, sparsely squamulate toward the base; primary squamules small, incised, often well developed; pycnidia common, apothecia rather rare, dark brown. P+ red (fumarprotocetraric acid). Widespread on sandy soil or humus in open areas. This rather undistinguished species is very similar to *C. cylindrica*, which differs chiefly in producing grayanic acid as well as fumarprotocetraric. *C. pityrea* has ecorticate bare areas.

48b Soredia more granular, scattered, bare ecorticate patches visible; eastern and northern North America. 49

49a Podetia usually small, sometimes irregular and twisted, more or less free of squamules. Fig. 302. ....
....*Cladonia pityrea* (**Flk.**) **Fr.**

Podetia whitish mineral gray, 0.5-1.5 cm high, with diffuse coarse soredia and tiny squamules but extensive ecorticate areas developing; primary squamules sparse, tiny, incised; apothecia rare. P+ red (fumarprotocetraric acid). Widespread on soil, old logs, and the base of trees in open woods. There is a great range of variation in production of soredia and squamules. When poorly developed, this *Cladonia* is hard to separate from *C. coniocraea* and other species with pointed podetia. A useful character to distinguish it would be the tinier incised squamules, almost identical with those of *C. squamosa.*

Figure 302.

49b Podetia larger, more or less squamulose. Fig. 303. ....
....*Cladonia decorticata* (Flk.) Spreng.

Podetia whitish mineral gray, 1.5-3.0 cm high, sparingly branched in the upper parts, sorediate, the soredia granular and intergrading with areoles or tiny squamules; primary squamules medium-sized; apothecia and pycnidia rare, dark brown. Widespread on soil or humus in conifer forests or open areas. P— (perlatolic acid). *C. cylindrica* is similar but lacks squamules on the podeta and is P+ red. *C. acuminata* (Ach.) Norrl.

Figure 303.

(K+ yellow→red, norstictic acid present) and *C. norrlinii* Vain. (K+ yellow, atranorin, and a P+ yellow unknown) are scarcely distinguishable rare chemical variants in the northern forests.

50a Podetia yellowish. Fig. 304. ....*Cladonia cyanipes* (Somm.) Nyl.

Podetia 2-5 cm tall, sparingly branched and sorediate in the upper parts, squamulate toward the base; primary squamules medium-sized to small, not well developed; pycnidia common, apothecia very rare, dark brown. Widespread on humus, rotting logs, and soil in open areas and bogs. This species is very similar to *C. cornuta* in appearance but differs in chemistry.

Figure 304.

50b Podetia whitish to greenish mineral gray or brownish. 51

51a Large areas corticate toward the base; soredia mostly toward tips. Fig. 305. .... *Cladonia cornuta* (**L.**) **Hoffm.**

Podetia greenish to brownish mineral gray, 3-8 cm tall, sparsely squamulate, infrequently branched; primary squamules medium-sized, poorly developed or absent; pycnidia and apothecia rare, dark brown. P+ red (fumarprotocetraric acid). Widespread on humus or among mosses over rocks in open areas. The elongate thin podetia resemble forms of *C. gracilis*, which lacks soredia.

Figure 305.

51b Soredia occurring over most of the podetial surface. 52

52a Podetia usually dichotomously branched. Fig. 306. ....
....*Cladonia scabriuscula* (**Duby**) **Leight.**

Podetia light mineral gray, 5-8 cm tall, sparsely to densely covered with squamules, moderately sorediate, especially in the upper parts; primary squamules poorly developed or absent; pycnidia common, apothecia very rare. P+ red (fumarprotocetraric acid). Widespread on soil in open pastures. Formerly confused with the more common *C. farinacea*, this species has fewer

Figure 306.

soredia and numerous squamules on the podetia. *C. subulata* (L.) Wigg., a rare northern species, differs chiefly in having almost entirely sorediate podetia.

52b Podetia irregularly branched to furcate. Fig. 307. ....
....*Cladonia farinacea* (**Vain.**) **Evans**

Podetia light mineral gray, 3-10 cm tall, sparingly branched with open axils; becoming sparsely squamulose toward the base; soredia farinose, diffuse over much of the surface; primary squamules small, dissected; apothecia rare, dark brown. P+ red (fumarprotocetraric acid). Common on soil and mossy rocks in pastures and along roadsides. *C. glauca* Flk.,

Figure 307.

which occurs only as far south as Connecticut, is very similar except for chemistry (P− squamatic acid). *C. scabriuscula* has granular, sparser soredia and more numerous squamules but shares the same P+ red reaction.

53a Podetia simple to branched, usually well developed. 54

53b Podetia barely developed, very short, or lacking and only large sterile squamules collected. 66

54a Podetia more or less richly branched, apothecia rare. Fig. 308.
....*Cladonia furcata* (**Huds.**) **Schrad.**

Podetia greenish to brownish mineral gray, sparsely squamulate, the axils open, sometimes expanding into narrow irregular cups, 4-8 cm tall; primary squamules sparsely developed to lacking; pycnidia common, apothecia rare, dark brown. P+ red (fumarprotocetraric acid). Very common on mossy rocks and humus in mature forests and fields or along roadsides. This will be collected very frequently and because of the great range of variability in size and in the development of squamules

Figure 308.

on the podetia some practice will be needed for positive identification. Three rare chemical variants are known in the northern part of the range: *C. pseudorangiformis* Asah. ·(atranorin, merochlorophaeic and psoromic acids), *C. rangiformis* Hoffm. (atranorin and rangiformic acid), and *C. subrangiformis* Sandst. (atranorin and fumarprotocetraric acid).

54b Podetia usually simple or sparingly branched, sometimes tipped with large apothecia. 55

55a Squamules lacking, the primary thallus crustose; podetia short
and inflated. Fig. 309. ....*Cladonia papillaria* (Ehrh.) Hoffm.

Figure 309.

Podetia light mineral gray, 0.5-1.5 cm tall, irregularly inflated and becoming branched, often constricted at the base; primary thallus granular, scattered; pycnidia common, apothecia rare. Common on sandy soil in open woods and along roadsides. No other *Cladonia* has this kind of primary thallus and inflated podetia. This species can also be classified in the genus *Pycnothelia*.

55b Squamules usually abundant, podetia not inflated. 56

56a Surface of podetia finely and densely squamulose (use hand
lens). ....*Cladonia squamosa* (see p. 156)

56b Surface of podetia free of squamules or coarsely squamulose. 57

57a Podetia and squamules with a yellowish cast (usnic acid present). Fig. 310. ....*Cladonia piedmontensis* Merr.

Figure 310.

Podetia 1-3 cm tall, sparingly branched, moderately squamulate over most of the surface; primary squamules medium-sized, usually well developed; pycnidia and apothecia common, brown. Common on sandy soil in open woods and along roadbanks. No other Cladonias in eastern United States have consistently well developed yellow podetia capped with apothecia.

57b Podetia and squamules whitish to greenish mineral gray. 58

58a Primary squamules large, 2-8 mm long, entire. 59

58b Primary squamules smaller or nearly lacking, 0.5-2.0 mm long,
usually dissected or granular. 60

59a Podetia entire, firmly attached; apothecia well developed. Fig. 311. ....*Cladonia clavulifera* **Vain.**

Podetia greenish mineral gray, 1-2 cm tall, simple or sparingly branched toward the upper parts, sparsely squamulate; primary squamules well developed, medium-sized; apothecia very common, dark brown. P+ red (fumarprotocetraric acid). Widespread on soil along roadbanks or in open fields. Podetia are usually present but this common lichen may be collected only as extensive patches of squamules.

Figure 311.

Three common chemical variants will also be collected: *C. polycarpia* Merr. (K+ yellow, stictic and norstictic acids), *C. symphycarpia* Fr. (K–, P+ yellow, psoromic acid), and *C. subcariosa* (K+ yellow, norstictic acid).

59b Podetia lacerated and perforate, often loosely growing; apothecia rare. Fig. 312. ....*Cladonia turgida* **(Ehrh.) Hoffm.**

Podetia aborted to well developed, loosely attached, to 5 cm tall, moderately branched with axils expanding into irregular cups, sparsely squamulate; primary squamules large, 1-3 cm long, dense, chalky white on the lower surface; pycnidia common, apothecia rare, dark brown. K+ yellow (atranorin), P– or P+ red (fumarprotocetraric acid). Widespread on humus or soil over rocks

Figure 312.

in open areas. The squamules are often so well developed as to be taller than the podetia.

60a Primary thallus of granules or very tiny squamules. 61

60b Primary thallus distinctly squamulose; squamules small to medium-sized. 62

61a Podetia tipped with large pale tan apothecia. Fig. 313. ....
....*Cladonia capitata* (**Michx.**) **Spreng.**

Figure 313.

Podetia mineral gray, 1.0-1.5 cm high, sparingly branched, with small dispersed corticate areas partially covering twisted, cartilaginous ribs; primary squamules very small, poorly developed; apothecia conspicuous. P+ red (fumarprotocetraric acid). Common on soil or at the base of trees in mature forests. The pale brown apothecia are diagnostic for this common *Cladonia*. *C. cariosa*, a northern species, has similar capitate apothecia but they are dark brown.

61b Podetia blunt, irregularly inflated, without apothecia ....
....*Cladonia papillaria* (see p. 166)

62a Podetia mostly free of squamules, tipped with large apothecia. 63

62b Podetia squamulose, apothecia often not present. 64

63a Podetia 1 cm or more tall, longitudinally ridged. Fig. 314.......
....*Cladonia cariosa* (**Ach.**) **Spreng.**

Figure 314.

Podetia whitish mineral gray, 1.5-2.5 cm tall, the surface with scattered areoles partially covering the ribbed medulla; primary squamules small, sparsely developed; apothecia conspicuous, dark brown. K+, P+ yellowish (stictic acid). Common on soil in open fields and along road cuts. While sometimes confused with *C. capitata*, *C. cariosa* has much darker apothecia and the podetia are not noticeably twisted.

63b Podetia less than 1 cm tall, the surface smooth. Fig. 315. ....
....*Cladonia botrytes* (**Hag.**) **Willd.**

Figure 315.

Podetia light mineral gray, 0.3-0.6 cm tall, sparingly branched in the upper part; primary squamules scattered, tiny; apothecia very common, tan or flesh-colored. Widespread but never abundant on rotting logs and stumps in open woods.

64a Collected in alpine-arctic localities. Fig. 316. ....
....*Cladonia macrophylla* **(Ehrh.) Ach.**

Podetia whitish mineral gray, 2-4 cm
high, sparingly branched in the upper
parts, densely areolate-squamulate but
conspicuous ridged cartilaginous areas
visible; primary squamules medium-
sized, scattered; pycnidia common,
apothecia rare, dark brown. P+ yellow
(psoromic acid). Widespread on soil
and humus in exposed areas. The
rather irregular often gnarled podetia
are characteristic of the species. *Cla-
donia squamosa* can be separated by a P– reaction and lack of
medulla ridges.

Figure 316.

64b Collected in eastern United States. 65

65a Primary squamules well developed; podetia sparingly branched.
Fig. 317. ....*Cladonia beaumontii* **Tuck.**

Podetia whitish mineral gray, 0.5-1.5 cm
tall, covered with tiny squamules; primary
squamules well developed, medium-sized,
incised; pycnidia and apothecia rare,
brown. P+ yellow (baeomycic and squamatic acids). On sandy soil, rotten logs,
and base of trees in open areas. A rare
companion species is *C. santensis* Tuck.,
which has smaller podetia (up to 0.8 cm)
and reacts K+ yellow (thamnolic acid).

Figure 317.

65b Primary squamules lacking; podetia becoming moderately
branched. ....*Cladonia squamosa* **(see p. 156)**

66a Apothecia short-stalked (1-2 mm high) or sessile on the squa-
mules (under hand lens). 67

66b Podetia and apothecia lacking, only large squamules present.
....*Squamulose Lichens* **(see Key V, p. 203)**

67a Squamules finely divided and incised. Fig. 318. ....
....*Cladonia caespiticia* (Pers.) Flk.

Podetia very tiny, up to 0.1 cm tall; primary squamules 0.3-0.5 cm long, incised, forming a dense mat; apothecia common, dark brown. P+ red (fumarprotocetraric acid). Common on rotting logs and on mosses over rocks in shady woods. When sterile, the squamules can be confused with either *C. parasitica* (K+ deep yellow) or aborted *C. squamosa* (K–, P–).

Figure 318.

67b Margins of squamules entire, not finely divided. 68

68a Squamules with a yellowish cast above and on the lower surface (usnic acid present); K–, P–, Fig. 319. ....
....*Cladonia robbinsii* Evans

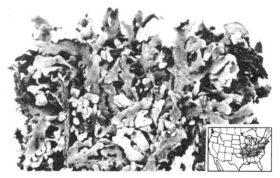

Figure 319. (X2).

Podetia rarely present, about 1 cm tall, irregularly cup-shaped; primary squamules well developed, strap-shaped, about 0.5 cm long, forming mats 3-6 cm broad, the lower surface cream to faint yellowish buff; apothecia rare, dark brown. Widespread on open soil or over rocks. The greenish yellow color will distinguish this rather rare lichen from other sterile *Cladonia* mats except for *C. strepsilis,* which forms more compact colonies and reacts C+ green.

68b Squamules greenish mineral gray to brownish, lower surface chalky white to brownish. 69

69a Lower surface of squamules K+ yellow or yellow→red. 70

69b Lower surface of squamules K— or K+ brownish. 72

70a Squamules very long (2-3 cm) and narrow with a blackened
base. ....Gymnoderma lineare (see p. 205)

70b Squamules shorter, broad, up to 1 cm long, the base not
blackened. 71

71a Lower surface of squamules K+ yellow→red. Fig. 320. ....
....Cladonia subcariosa Nyl.

Podetia commonly not developed, simple
to sparingly branched, 0.5-1.5 cm high; primary squamules well developed, greenish
mineral gray, strap-shaped, up to 1 cm long,
the lower surface white to buff, forming
extensive mats; apothecia common. K+ yel-
low→red, P+ orange (norstictic acid). Common on soil in abandoned fields, open
woods, and along roadsides. This is probably
the most frequently collected sterile Cladonia on open soil. C. polycarpia and C.
clavulifera, however, are very close and
would have to be distinguished by crystal
tests.   Figure 320.

71b Squamules persistently K+ yellow. ....
.... Cladonia turgida (see p. 167)

72a Lower surface of squamules chalky white, C—; colonies scattered. Fig. 321. ....Cladonia apodocarpa Robb.

Podetia lacking; primary squamules greenish mineral gray, large and strap-shaped,
about 1 cm long, suberect with the white
lower surface visible; apothecia rare, borne
on tiny stipes on the squamules. P+ red
(fumarprotocetraric acid). Very common on
sandy soil in open woods or along roadsides.
This is usually collected as sterile squamules.
Closely related sterile species such as C. sub-   Figure 321.
cariosa, C. clavulifera, and C. mateocyatha
will have to be separated by appropriate chemical tests, although
in general the strap-shaped suberect squamules of C. apodocarpa
are easy to recognize. In the western states, Lecidea novomexicana
B. de Lesd. has similar but more rounded squamules and larger
adnate apothecia.

72b Lower surface cream to brownish, C+, KC+ green; colonies often forming compact balls or mats. Fig. 322. ....
.... *Cladonia strepsilis* (Ach.) Vain.

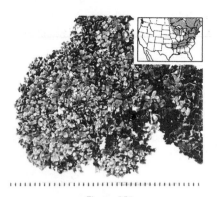

Podetia rarely developed, irregularly cup-shaped, up to 1 cm tall, primary squamules well developed, yellowish to greenish gray, the lower surface whitish to cream, often forming compact mats or balls 4-6 cm broad; apothecia very rare, dark brown. C+ green (strepsilin), P+ yellow (baeomycic acid). Widespread on soil in open areas and between boulders at large outcrops. The most unusual feature is the C+ green reaction, but the growth habit alone is diagnostic. *C. robbinsii* has a similar color but differs chemically. *C. apodocarpa* has longer squamules chalky white below.

Figure 322.

73a Crustose primary thallus present; apothecia on short stalks (0.5-2.0 cm high). *Baeomyces, Pilophoron.* 74

73b Primary thallus (crust or squamules) completely lacking; apothecia (if present) not stalked. 78

74a Apothecia pink to pale brown, often flattened. 75

74b Apothecia black, rounded to elongate. 77

75a Apothecia large, orbicular, pink. Fig. 323. ....
.... *Baeomyces roseus* Pers.

Pseudopodetia white, 0.3-0.6 cm tall, unbranched; primary thallus crustose, granular, whitish mineral gray; apothecia common, rounded, light pink. P+ yellow (baeomycic acid). Common on soil along open roadbanks. The primary crust consolidates freshly exposed soil and soon produces the attractive pink apothecia. Rarer *B. absolutus* also has pink but much smaller and peltate apothecia.

Figure 323.

75b Apothecia small and flattened, brown or pinkish. 76

76a Thallus thin and greenish. Fig. 324. ....
....*Baeomyces absolutus* **Tuck.**

Pseudopodetia white, 0.1-0.3 cm high;
primary thallus thin, greenish, smooth;
apothecia pink. P+ yellow (baeomycic
acid). Rare on rocks in mature forests.
B. rufus (Huds.) Rebent., common on
rocks and soil in northern and western
United States, is similar but has a grayish
thallus and reacts K+ yellow (stictic
acid).

Figure 324.

76b Thallus thicker, granular to subsquamulose. Fig. 325. ....
....*Baeomyces carneus* **Flk.**

Pseudopodetia brownish mineral gray,
0.2-0.5 cm tall; primary thallus forming a
rather thick crust, 3-8 cm broad; apothecia common, peltate, dark brown. K+,
P+ yellow (norstictic acid). Rare on
boulders in open forests. This species is
inconspicuous and difficult to collect from
flat granitic rocks. In arctic regions one
will find *B. placophyllus* Ach., which has
a very thick almost lobate thallus.

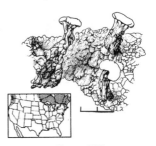

Figure 325.

77a Apothecia rather elongate. Fig. 326. ....
....*Pilophoron hallii* (Tuck.) **Vain.**

Podetia greenish mineral gray, 0.5-1.5 cm tall,
unbranched; primary thallus more or less continuous, composed of granules or areoles; apothecia
common, black. K | yellow (atranorin). Common
on rocks in moist woods.

Figure 326.

77b Apothecia rounded. Fig. 327. ....

.... *Pilophoron aciculare* **(Ach.) Nyl.**

Figure 327.

Pseudopodetia light mineral gray, slender, 1-3 cm tall, sparingly branched in the upper parts; primary thallus granular or minutely areolate; apothecia very common, black. Common on rocks in open woods and along streams. This is probably the most frequently collected *Pilophoron*. In alpine districts of eastern North America one will find *P. cereolus* (Ach.) Nyl., which also has rounded apothecia but the pseudopodetia are only 0.1-0.3 cm high.

78a Thallus (or apothecia) orange, K+ purple (parietin). 79
78b Thallus not orange. 80
79a Thallus tufted, branches flattened, 1-2 cm long, with ciliate apothecia. Fig. 328. ....

....*Teloschistes chrysophthalmus* **(L.) Th. Fr.**

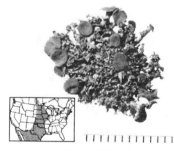

Figure 328.

Thallus mineral gray, tufted, 1-2 cm broad, loosely attached; branches flattened, little branched but becoming spinulate or ciliate marginally; apothecia very common, the rim spinulate. Widespread on exposed trees or on branches at the tops of trees. This colorful lichen is smaller than *T. exilis* and apparently more common.

79b Thallus not tufted, branches rounded in cross section; apothecia eciliate or lacking. Fig. 329. ....

.... *Teloschistes exilis* **(Michx.) Vain.**

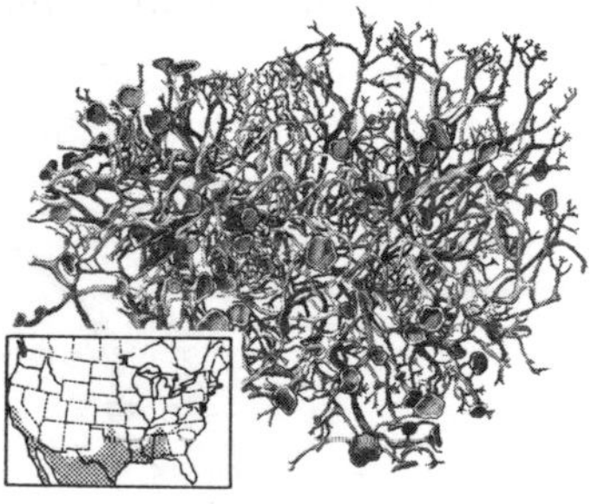

Thallus pale to deep orange, 3-7 cm broad, loosely attached; branches flattened to round, becoming finely spinulate at the tips; apothecia common. Common on exposed trees in prairie regions or open dry uplands. A closely related but rarer species, *T. flavicans* (Sw.) Ach., is sorediate and lacks apothecia.

Figure 329.

Thallus 4-12 cm long, more or less suberect; surface distinctly ridged and pitted (under a hand lens), turning sorediate; apothecia common, the rim often dentate (vulpinic acid present). Common in conifer forests. This brilliant lichen often occurs on the California redwoods. The nonsorediate form is sometimes called a separate species, *L. californica* (Lév.) Hue.

Figure 330.

Thallus bright greenish yellow, 3-5 cm tall, growing erect among mosses or on humus; surface shiny, smooth to faintly rugose and pitted; base sometimes turning dark purple red; pycnidia very common, tiny, apothecia rare. Widespread in arctic and arctic-alpine regions. Closely related *C. nivalis* (L.) Ach., which has more flattened and deeply rugose lobes, frequently occurs with this species. *C. tilesii* Ach. differs in having a deep lemon or orange yellow thallus (vulpinic acid); it will be found in the high Rockies.

Figure 331.

85a Soredia granular to subisidiate, scattered over the thallus; branches flattened to irregularly rounded, limp. Fig. 332. ......
....*Evernia mesomorpha* Nyl.

Figure 332.

Thallus pale greenish yellow, prostrate to pendulous, soft and flabby, 4-6 cm long; surface irregularly wrinkled; apothecia very rare (divaricatic acid present). Common on conifers, fenceposts, and shingles in the northern forests. Lack of fibrils and the irregularly thickened branches easily separate it from *Usnea*.

85b Soredia in distinct soralia, usually marginal or apical; branches flattened, rarely rounded, usually leathery or brittle. 86

86a Branches flattened to rounded, hollow and usually perforate, especially toward the base (under hand lens). Fig. 333. ....
....*Ramalina roesleri* (Hochst.) Nyl.

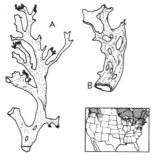

Figure 333. A, thallus (X4); B, perforations (X10).

Thallus pale yellowish green, tufted, 1-4 cm long; branches dense and attenuate toward the tips, moderately isidiate-sorediate; apothecia very rare. Widespread on branches of conifers in open areas but not abundant. The hollow perforate branches may be overlooked in this inconspicuous little lichen.

86b Branches more or less flattened throughout, solid and imperforate. 87

87a Tips of lobes bursting open, sorediate. Fig. 334. ....
.... *Ramalina pollinaria* (**Westr.**) **Ach.**

Thallus pale yellowish green, tufted, 1-2 cm long; soredia diffuse, forming over the exposed medulla; apothecia very rare (evernic acid present). Rare on tree trunks and sandstone outcrops in fairly sheltered areas. The species is easily recognized by the broad white sorediate patches. In California there is a very similar but larger species, *R. evernioides* Nyl., which contains an unidentified acid.

Figure 334.

87b Tips of lobes entire, soralia mostly along the margins. 88

88a Thallus growing on rocks. Fig. 335. ....
....*Ramalina intermedia* **Nyl.**

Thallus yellowish green, tufted but often forming extensive colonies, 1-3 cm long; branches becoming finely divided; apothecia very rare. Common on large boulders or overhanging cliffs in exposed areas, rarely on trees. This is probably part of a large group of microspecies, which differ in chemistry and minor morphological characters, but they have not yet been carefully studied.

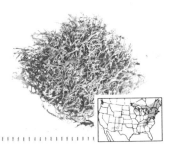

Figure 335.

88b Thallus growing on trees. 89

89a Thallus rather flabby; surface rugose and pitted. Fig. 336. ......
....*Evernia prunastri* (**L.**) **Ach.**

Thallus pale yellowish green, tufted, 2-7 cm long; branches rather wide, paler on the lower surface; apothecia unknown (evernic acid present). Common on trunks and branches of trees and on fenceposts in open areas or in bogs. Though very common from California to Washington, this is a rarity in eastern North America, where *E. meso-morpha* is far more common.

Figure 336.

89b Thallus more rigid; surface shiny, smooth or longitudinally striate. Fig. 337. .... *Ramalina farinacea* (**L.**) **Ach.**

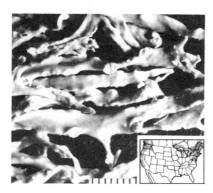

Figure 337.

Thallus pale yellowish green, tufted to pendulous, 3-7 cm long; branches sparsely divided except toward the tips; apothecia very rare. Medulla K— or K+ yellow, P— or P+ red (with or without salacinic or protocetraric acids). Widespread on tree trunks, rarely on rocks, in open areas. This variable species is poorly known and appears to have several chemical races. A very large plant in California and Oregon appears to be the sorediate form of *R. leptocarpa* (see p. 181). In southern United States one may find *R. peruviana* Ach., a more delicate richly branched sorediate species.

90a Branches and apothecia with long black cilia. Fig. 338. ....*Ramalina crinita* **Tuck.**

Figure 338.

Thallus pale greenish yellow, tufted, 3-6 cm long; apothecia very common. On shrubs in open areas. This strange endemic species is the only ciliate *Ramalina* in North America.

90b Cilia completely lacking. **91**

91a Thallus pendulous, 10-40 cm long, branches twisted, becoming net-like. Fig. 339. ......*Ramalina reticulata* (**Noehd.**) **Kremplh.**

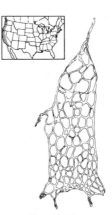

Thallus greenish yellow, pendulous on tree branches, branches variable in width, becoming expanded and perforated like a net; apothecia very rare. Very common on oak trees in open areas. This unmistakable lichen drapes trees heavily and is often collected on scrub oaks in California. A similar pendulous species without development of perforations is *R. usnea* (L.) Howe which occurs in southern Florida, Texas, and Mexico.

Figure 339.

91b Thallus branches entire, tufted and suberect, not twisted or net-like. 92

92a Branches leathery, without papillae, pitted and rugose, sparsely branched, often collected on rocks. 93

92b Branches thinner, rather fragile, often papillate or striate but not rugose, collected on trees. 94

93a Branches becoming rounded, without transverse cracks. Fig. 340. ....*Ramalina combeoides* Nyl.
Thallus greenish yellow, tufted, rather fragile, 2-4 cm long; branches simple or sparingly branched; apothecia very common, terminal. Common in exposed habitats near the ocean. A frequent companion species, *R. ceruchis* (Ach.) De Not., is larger (4-6 cm long), occurs on shrubs as well as rocks, and has mostly lateral apothecia. It contains evernic acid and with age becomes covered with a white cottony excrescence that looks like a white mold.

Figure 340.

93b Branches strongly flattened and transversely cracked. Fig. 341.
....*Ramalina homalea* **Ach.**

Thallus greenish yellow, turning brownish in the herbarium, blackening at the base, tufted, leathery, 4-10 cm long; surface becoming ridged and cracked; apothecia common, lateral (divaricatic acid present). Common on rocks, especially along the seashore. It is often collected with *R. combeoides*, which is usually smaller and with rounded branches.

Figure 341.

94a Branches generally broad, 2-10 mm wide. 95
94b Branches narrow, 1 mm or less. 97
95a Branches with numerous laminal apothecia. Fig. 342. ....
....*Ramalina ecklonii* **(Spreng.) Mey. & Flot.**

Thallus greenish yellow, tufted, membranous, 4-8 cm long; surface longitudinally deeply striate; apothecia numerous. Common on branches and trunks of deciduous trees in open areas. The laminal apothecia distinguish this conspicuous lichen from the *R. fastigiata* group.

Figure 342. (X1/2).

95b Branches with terminal apothecia. 96
96a Surface of branches smooth to striate. Fig. 343. ....
....*Ramalina fastigiata* **(Pers.) Ach.**

Thallus greenish yellow, tufted, 1-4 cm long; branches quite variable in width, 2-10 mm wide; surface striate, rarely perforate; apothecia common, spores ellipsoid. Common on tree trunks in open areas and on branches in the canopy. This name covers a large and extremely variable group of species that are poorly known. *R. sinensis* Jatta, *R. fraxinea* (L.) Ach.,

Figure 343.

and *R. subamplicata* (Nyl.) Fink are names used for very broad-lobed specimens but intergradations with narrow forms are numerous and difficult to describe. A long linear-lobed form in California with subterminal apothecia is called *R. leptocarpa* Tuck. A similar form along the Gulf Coast, *R. stenospora* Müll. Arg., has fusiform spores but intergrades with *R. willeyi* (see p. 182).

(see p. 182)

96b Surface of branches strongly papillate or papillate-striate. Fig. 344. ....*Ramalina complanata* (**Sw.**) **Ach.**

Thallus pale greenish yellow, tufted, leathery, 2-3 cm long; apothecia numerous, terminal (divaricatic acid present). Common on tree trunks and branches in open woods and along roadsides. Since the coarse papillae are distinct and whitish, there should be little confusion with *R. fastigiata*, which has a thinner thallus and low striae rather than papillae. *R. denticulata* Nyl., another southern papillate species, has salacinic acid (K+ red) and a generally larger thallus (3-5 cm) with narrower lobes.

Figure 344.

97a Thallus 1-2 cm tall; branches in part inflated and hollow (under hand lens). Fig. 345. ....*Ramalina minuscula* (**Nyl.**) **Nyl.**

Thallus greenish yellow, tufted; branches becoming rounded, rather richly branched; apothecia common, mostly lateral. On branches of trees in open areas, rare but probably overlooked. A tubular sparsely branched form, *R. inflata* Hook. & Tayl., occurs in the western states. There are several other species in this group which are still poorly known.

Figure 345.

97b **Thallus 2-6 cm tall; branches solid. Fig. 346.** ....
....*Ramalina willeyi* **Howe**

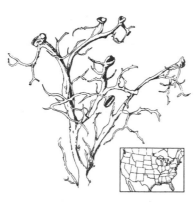

Figure 346. (X2).

Thallus greenish yellow, tufted; branches narrow, becoming rounded, finely divided, the surface longitudinally striate; apothecia common, mostly subterminal or lateral, spores ellipsoid. Medulla K+ red, P+ orange (salacinic acid or if K− protocetraric acid). Common on shrubs and tree branches in the Coastal Plain. There are three closely related species that have nearly the same range: *R. tenuis* (Tuck.) Merr. with thinner attenuated branches; *R. montagnei* De Not. with fusiform spores; and *R. stenospora* Müll. Arg. with strongly flattened branches and fusiform spores.

98a **Thallus tufted, 3-10 cm long (up to 20 cm in** *Usnea ceratina* **and** *U. dasypoga*) **firmly attached at the base to the substratum (loose on soil only in** *Agrestia*). 99

98b **Thallus pendulous, 10-50 cm long, usually growing draped on tree branches and without a distinct base.** 111

99a **Thallus growing on soil in the Great Plains. Fig. 347.** ....
....*Agrestia hispida* (**Oxn.**) **Thoms.**

Figure 347.

Thallus dark greenish or olive yellow, prostrate, brittle, 1-2 cm broad; branches spinulate, irregularly thickened, with white pores; apothecia rare, sessile to immersed. Widespread in the Great Plains. Long overlooked, this unusual lichen is apparently a common component of the prairie soil vegetation.

99b Thallus growing on bark or rock. 100

100a Soredia and isidia lacking (use lens) (there may be numerous short fibrils); apothecia common. 101

100b Soredia and/or isidia present; apothecia rare. 103

101a Branches densely fibrillose. Fig. 348. ....
....*Usnea strigosa* (Ach.) Eaton

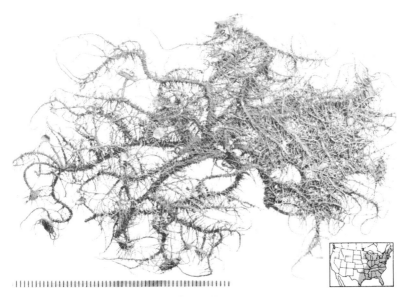

Figure 348.

Thallus greenish yellow, tufted, 3-8 cm long; branches moderately papillate; medulla rusty red or rose, especially toward the tips of branches, or pigment lacking; apothecia very common. Medulla K— or K+ red, P— or P+ yellow or orange (usnic acid alone or with norstictic and galbinic acids or psoromic or fumarprotocetraric acids). Common on canopy branches of deciduous trees and exposed trunks. There are several species in this variable group which are difficult to identify. *U. subfusca* Stirt. has salacinic acid and numerous papillae and occurs in the Appalachian Mountains. *U. arizonica* Mot. also apparently has salacinic acid and is common in the southwestern states. *U. evansii* Mot. and *U. tristis* Mot. are merely variants of *U. strigosa*.

101b Fibrils lacking. 102

102a Branches with distinct white medulla, stiff (use razor blade). ....*Ramalina willeyi* (see p. 182)

102b Branches very thin and hair-like, soft, medulla lacking. Fig. 349. ....*Coenogonium interplexum* Nyl.

Figure 349.

Thallus dull yellowish green, forming mats 1-3 cm wide, the branches up to 0.5 cm long; algal component *Trentepohlia;* apothecia common, pale yellow, spores colorless, uniseriate, 1-septate, 2-3 x 6-9μ. Common at the base of trees in mature forests. There are four other common species in this genus which must be separated with a microscope: *C. moniliforme* Tuck. has branches divided like a chain of pearls; *C. interpositum* Nyl. has simple biseriate spores; *C. linkii* Ehrenb. has a shelf-like thallus with 1-septate biseriate spores; and *C. implexum* Nyl. has uniseriate spores 2-4 x 7-12μ.

103a Medulla rusty red or rose (expose with razor blade under lens). Fig. 350. .... *Usnea mutabilis* Stirt.

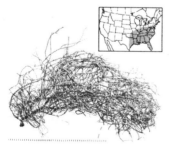

Figure 350.

Thallus greenish yellow, tufted, 2-8 cm long; branches moderately papillate and isidiate-spinulate, the papillae becoming sorediate; apothecia lacking. Common on trunks of deciduous trees in open woods. This is apparently the isidiate-sorediate form of *U. strigosa.*

103b Medulla uniformly white (cortex at base may be reddish). 104

104a Soredia powdery in orbicular soralia. Fig. 351. ....
....*Usnea fulvoreagens* (Räs.) Räs.

Thallus greenish yellow, tufted, 3-10 cm long; branches papillate, with large soralia; apothecia rare. Medulla K+ yellow, P+ orange (salacinic acid). Common on trees in open woods and along roadsides. The chemistry is variable, and some specimens may contain norstictic or stictic acids instead of salacinic. There are a number of microspecies (*U. betulina* Mot., *U. laricina* Vain.) but it is beyond the scope of this book to separate these.

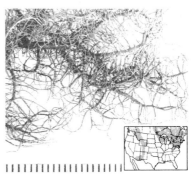

Figure 351.

104b Soredia diffuse and becoming isidiate or only isidia present.
....**105**

105a Branches (toward the base) with a hollow central cord (section carefully with razor blade). Fig. 352. ....
....*Usnea antillarum* (Vain.) Zahlbr.

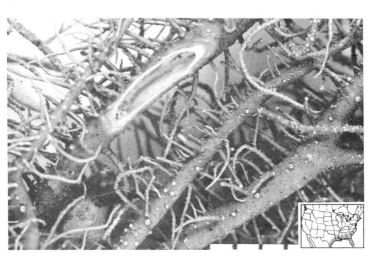

Figure 352.

Thallus greenish yellow, tufted, rather stiff, basal branches inflated, 5-10 cm long; branches papillate, becoming densely sorediate-isidiate and isidiate; medulla turning reddish; apothecia lacking. Medulla K+ yellowish, (unknown substances). Rare on trees in open woods. The hollow branches may not be noticed at first and the specimens will probably be identified as *U. comosa* or *U. mutabilis*. Two rarer southern Usneas have hollow branches: *U. implicita* Stirt. (base not inflated) and *U. vainioi* Mot. (sorediate without isidia).

105b Branches with a dense solid central cord. 106

106a Branches without papillae, relatively long and sparsely divided, densely sorediate-isidiate. Fig. 353. ....
....*Usnea hirta* (L.) Wigg.

Thallus dark greenish yellow, tufted, flabby, 3-6 cm long; branches mostly smooth, papillae rare or lacking, densely fibrillose, in part sorediate-isidiate, the isidia long; apothecia lacking. Common on bark of trees in open areas. This species is not well defined and will be confused with *U. comosa* and others. *U. variolosa* Mot. is reported to differ in having very short isidia, but it is not really possible to separate these species.

Figure 353.

106b Branches with conspicuous papillae, soredia or isidia sparsely to moderately developed. 107

107a Base of thallus blackening, constricted. Fig. 354. ....
....*Usnea comosa* **(Ach.) Ach.**

Thallus greenish yellow, tufted 3-8 cm long; branches finely papillate, sorediate, the soralia becoming orbicular; apothecia lacking. Medulla K+ yellow, P+ orange (salacinic and usnic acids). Very common on trees in open woods. The constricted blackened base is the most important diagnostic character. There is apparently chemical variation, since some specimens contain protocetraric acid or squamatic acid.

Figure 354.

107b Base of thallus not blackening or constricted. **108**

108a Branches (especially toward the base) turning reddish. Fig. 355. ....*Usnea rubiginea* **(Michx.) Mass.**

Thallus dark greenish yellow to rusty red, tufted, 2-6 cm long; branches moderately papillate, the papillae becoming sorediate and isidiate-sorediate; apothecia lacking. Medulla K+ yellow, P+ yellow (stictic acid). Common on tree trunks and rocks in mature forests. The reddish color and presence of stictic acid immediately identify this common *Usnea*.

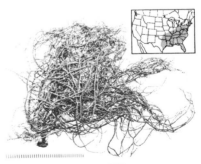

Figure 355.

108b Branches not turning color (rarely mottled reddish in U. dasypoga). **109**

109a Thallus growing on rocks, tufted, 3-8 cm long. Fig. 356. ....
....*Usnea herrei* **Hale**

Figure 356.

Thallus greenish yellow, rather stiff; branches short, with long fibrils, tending to fall in one direction, the cortex becoming reticulately rugose, papillate, the papillae sorediate and isidiate-sorediate; apothecia lacking. Medulla K+ yellow→red, P+ orange (norstictic acid). Common on exposed acidic rocks. The branching pattern and chemistry set this species apart. It is the commonest saxicolous *Usnea* in southeastern United States. Other related saxicolous species will be collected but their taxonomy is poorly known at present.

109b Thallus growing on trees, tufted or becoming pendulous, 6-20 cm long. **110**

110a Main branches coarsely papillate, richly branched. Fig. 357.
....*Usnea ceratina* **Ach.**

Figure 357. (X2).

Thallus greenish yellow, tufted to pendulous, 6-20 cm long; papillae becoming sorediate; apothecia rare (diffractaic acid present). Widespread on tree trunks in open woods. This species is not well known and is usually misidentified in herbaria. It is generally larger than species in the *U. comosa* or *U. fulvoreagens* groups.

110b Main branches finely papillate, with few secondary branches. Fig. 358. ....*Usnea dasypoga* **(Ach.) Nyl.**

Thallus greenish yellow, generally pendulous with long main branches, 10-20 cm long; branches turning sorediate and isidiate-sorediate; apothecia rare. Medulla K+ yellow →red, P+ orange (salacinic and usnic acids). Widespread in open woods. Size alone distinguishes this *Usnea*, but there is obvious intergradation with *U. ceratina* and other isidiate-sorediate species.

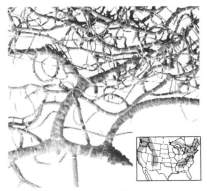

Figure 358.

111a Branches with numerous short lateral fibrils and branchlets. 112

111b Branches smooth, sparsely to richly branched but fibrils lacking. 113

112a Main branches with sharp angular ridges. Fig. 359. ....
.... *Usnea angulata* Ach.

Thallus dark greenish yellow pendulous, stiff, 15-25 cm long; main branch distinct, with short secondary branchlets, the branchlets papillate and sparsely sorediate; apothecia rare. Medulla K+ yellow, P+ yellowish (norstictic acid). Rare in tree tops. This *Usnea* is easy to identify but it is not only rare but difficult to collect in tall trees. In Florida there is a pendulous species with a smooth cortex and articulated branches called *U. dimorpha* Müll. Arg., which contains galbinic and norstictic acids. In the western states, *U. scabiosa* Mot. has a rugose cortex and numerous very short isidia-like fibrils.

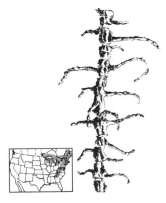

Figure 359. (X5).

112b Main branches whitened, smooth, the cortex eroding and decomposing. Fig. 360. .... *Usnea longissima* (L.) Ach.

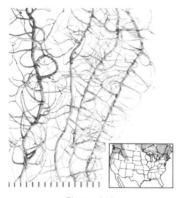

Thallus pale greenish yellow, pendulous, 15-30 cm long; main branches rugose, the cortex disappearing with age, the secondary branches with sparse soralia; apothecia very rare. (Barbatic acid present.) Rare on branches of conifers. This classical lichen is much less common than *U. cavernosa* or *U. trichodea*. There are other chemical variants but little is known of them.

Figure 360.

113a Branches solid, with a distinct central cord (use razor blade and hand lens). 114

113b Branches loosely filled with medullary tissue, a central cord lacking. 115

114a Base of main branches smooth. Fig. 361. ....
....*Usnea trichodea* Ach.

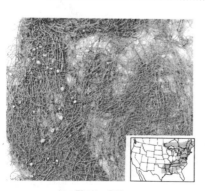

Thallus pale greenish yellow, pendulous, soft, 10-30 cm long; main branches cracked, annulate; apothecia common. Medulla K+ red or K− (salacinic acid, diffractaic or evernic acid). Widespread in tops of trees, often in swamps. In the southern forests this conspicuous lichen may be mistaken for Spanish Moss. *U. cavernosa* has a similar appearance but the main branches are entire and rugose.

Figure 361.

114b Base of main branches rugose and pitted. Fig. 362. ....
....*Usnea cavernosa* **Tuck.**

Figure 362.

Thallus pale greenish yellow, pendulous, soft, 10-30 cm long; branches continuous with long secondary branchlets; apothecia occasional. Medulla K+ yellow, P+ orange (unidentified substances). Common on trees in bogs and open areas. This is the most commonly collected pendulous *Usnea* in the northern states and Canada.

115a Isidiate soredia present. Fig. 363. .... *Alectoria crinalis* **Ach.**

Thallus dark greenish yellow, pendulous, 10-20 cm long; branches smooth, striate, with small clumps of isidiate soredia at the tips; apothecia lacking. Rare on conifers or deciduous trees. Unless the inconspicuous isidia are recognized, this will be misidentified as *Alectoria sarmentosa* or even an *Usnea*.

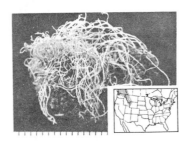

Figure 363.

115b Soredia lacking. Fig. 364. .... *Alectoria sarmentosa* (**Ach.**) **Ach.**

Figure 364.

Thallus greenish yellow, pendulous, rather stiff, 10-30 cm long; branches white striate, often becoming twisted; apothecia rare. Common on trees in mountainous areas. Beginners will invariably call this an *Usnea* but the branches lack a central cord. It is very common on fir trees in the Pacific Northwest. A rare more brownish yellow species with finer branches and no striae is *A. implexa* (Hoffm.) Nyl. which may be confused with *A. sarmentosa*. In arctic and alpine regions one will collect *A. ochroleuca* (Hoffm.) Mass., which is very similar to *A. sarmentosa* but has a dark greenish base. In Colorado a comparable tundra lichen is *Evernia perfragilis* Llano, a yellow short-branched brittle species with divaricatic acid. Also in the Rocky Mountains one may rarely find *E. divaricata* (L.) Ach., a flabby pendulous species on conifers, containing divaricatic acid.

116a Thallus brown or black. **117**

116b Thallus not brown or black. **125**

117a Thallus branches flattened (without lens). Fig. 365. Iceland Moss. ....*Cetraria islandica* (**L.**) **Ach.**

Figure 365.

Thallus greenish olive to brown, growing loosely on soil, the lobes 3-7 cm high, forming irregular colonies 5-20 cm broad; surface sparsely pseudocyphellate, with short ciliate margins; base sometimes turning red; apothecia very rare. Medulla P− or P+ deep red (protolichesterinic or if P+ fumarprotocetraric acid). On sandy soils in exposed areas. The P− population can be recognized as a distinct species, *C. ericetorum* Opiz. At high elevation from Washington to Alaska one may find a broad lobed form at the base of shrubs, *C. subalpina* Imsh.

Thallus chestnut brown, tufted to prostrate, 4-10 cm long; branches shiny; apothecia very rare. Medulla P+ red (fumarprotocetraric acid). Common on conifers and fenceposts in open areas. This species will be collected frequently and because of the isidiate soralia is quite distinct.

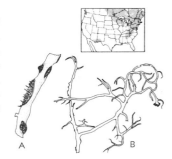

Figure 366. A (X10); B (X2).

Thallus dark chestnut brown, 8-20 cm long; branches sparse; soralia yellowish, capitate; apothecia very rare. Common on conifers throughout the western states. Other sorediate species that are P+ red will be collected. They are not only difficult to identify positively but intergrade with nonsorediate forms. *A. positiva* (Gyel.) Mot., for example, differs chiefly in being P | red. *A. simplicior* (Vain.) Lynge has a smaller thallus (3-6 cm) and very fine branches. *A. nadvornikiana* Gyel. is light brown overall with greater branching; it occurs widely in eastern North America.

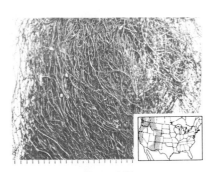

Figure 367.

120a Thallus pendulous, 10-30 cm long. Fig. 368. ....
....*Alectoria americana* **Mot.**

Figure 368. (X3)

Thallus dark chestnut brown, 10-30 cm long; branches smooth, very fine (about 0.5 mm wide); apothecia rare. Common on conifers in the boreal forest, becoming rare in relict bogs in the southern part of the range. This species is well known as "*A. jubata*" or "*A. chalybeiformis.*" The fine branches help in distinguishing it from abnormal nonsorediate forms of *A. fremontii.* A more yellowish brown species, *A. implexa* (Hoffm.) Nyl. (see p. 192), may also key out here.

120b Thallus not pendulous but more or less tufted or prostrate, 1-10 cm long. **121**

121a Branches 1-2 cm long, often tipped with apothecia (except for *Ephebe*). **122**

121b Branches 3-10 cm long, apothecia very rare. **124**

122a Thallus richly branched, collected on conifer bark. Fig. 369.
....*Alectoria oregana* **Tuck.**

Figure 369.

Thallus dark brown, prostrate to sub-erect, 1-3 cm high, irregularly branched and spinulate; apothecia common, the rim spinulate. Common on branches of conifers. The thallus is much smaller than that of any other Alectorias. *Cornicularia californica* (Tuck.) DR. is virtually indistinguishable except for flatter branches and more numerous spinules.

122b Thallus more sparsely branched, collected on rocks. 123

123a Branches 1 mm or more wide with a distinct white medulla
(use razor blade). Fig. 370. ....
...............................Cornicularia normoerica (Gunn.) DR.

Thallus blackish brown, suberect,
1.0-1.5 cm tall, sparingly branched;
apothecia common, terminal, the rim
dentate. Rare on exposed rocks. This
curious lichen is inconspicuous and
probably more common than the few
records indicate.

Figure 370.

123b Branches 0.5 mm or less wide, dark inside without a white
medulla. Fig. 371. ....Ephebe lanata (L.) Vain.
Thallus black, dull, tufted
and hair-like, flaccid, irregularly
branched, branches up to 1 cm
long and 70-140μ thick, forming
extensive mats on rock; hyphal
cells elongate, parallel, the algal
component Stigonema; apothecia
rare. Widespread on moist rocks,
especially near waterfalls. The algae make up most of the thallus.
Ephebe solida Born., a second
widespread species, is larger (up
to 2 cm), stiff, and dichotomously
branched, and has branches 130-
260μ thick. E. americana Henss.

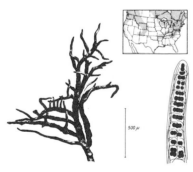

Figure 371.

has thin branches (40-55μ) but hyphae with angular cells arranged in irregular nets. All must be examined under the microscope.

124a Branches spinulate, brittle. Fig. 372. ....
....Cornicularia aculeata (Schreb.) Ach.

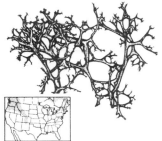

Thallus chestnut brown, erect on soil or humus, 3-6 cm tall; branches shiny, sparsely pitted and perforate; apothecia very rare (protolichesterinic acid present). Rare in sheltered areas in arctic or alpine localities. The spinulate branches distinguish it from *C. divergens* Ach., a larger, C+ red species, or arctic Alectorias.

Figure 372.

124b Branches lacking spinules, soft. Fig. 373. ....
....Alectoria bicolor (Ehrh.) Nyl.

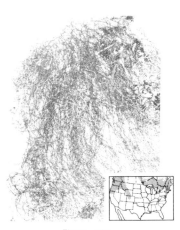

Thallus dark brown in the upper parts, turning tan toward the base, prostrate to suberect, 4-10 cm long; apothecia rare. Medulla P+ red (unknown substances). Common on soil and humus in arctic and alpine habitats. There are a number of difficult nonsorediate Alectorias in the arctic tundra, which is out of the range of this book. These should be identified with Motyka's monograph.

Figure 373.

125a Lower surface of branches channelled (see Fig. 403); thallus always collected on trees. 126

125b Branches round or if flat without a channelled lower surface. 128

126a Isidia present (use lens). Fig. 374. ....
................................*Pseudevernia consocians* **(Vain.) Hale & Culb.**

Thallus subfruticose, light mineral gray, loosely attached; 5-10 cm broad; upper surface moderately to densely isidiate; lower surface white to mottled black; apothecia very rare. Cortex K+ yellow (atranorin); medulla C+, KC+ red (lecanoric acid). Common on conifers in mountainous areas. In the Rocky Mountains most collections of this genus are *Pseudevernia intensa,* which lacks isidia. This lichen had previously been called *Parmelia furfuracea,* a very similar European lichen with physodic or olivetoric acid.

Figure 374.

126b Isidia lacking. **127**

127a Collected in the Appalachian Mountains. Fig. 375. ....
................*Pseudevernia cladonia* **(Tuck.) Hale & Culb.**

Thallus fruticose, suberect on twigs, light mineral gray, 4-10 cm broad; branches somewhat dorsiventral; lower surface white to mottled black, naked; apothecia very rare. Cortex K+ yellow (atranorin); medulla C+ red, KC+ red (lecanoric acid). Common on conifers at high elevations (4-6000 ft.). *Pseudevernia consocians* commonly occurs with it but has isidia and much wider branches. This lichen too was formerly classified as a *Parmelia,* but *Parmelia* is characterized by rhizines below.

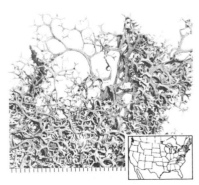

Figure 375.

127b Collected in western North America. Fig. 376. ....
.... *Pseudevernia intensa* (**Nyl.**) **Hale & Culb.**

Thallus light mineral gray, loosely attached on bark, 5-10 cm broad; upper surface smooth to deeply wrinkled, black pycnidia common; lower surface black at the center but usually turning mottled buff to white at the margin; apothecia common. Cortex K+ yellow (atranorin); medulla C+, KC+ red (lecanoric acid). Common on exposed conifers. This species has usually not been separated from *P. consocians*, which may occur with it in Mexico.

Figure 376.

128a Branches flat; collected in southern California. 129

128b Branches round; collected in temperate and boreal North America. 130

129a Thallus conspicuously sorediate. Fig. 377. ....
.... *Roccella babingtonii* **Mont.**

Figure 377.

Thallus white to light mineral gray, 4-8 cm long, leathery, tufted to pendulous on trees or rocks; surface sorediate, the soralia capitate; apothecia very rare. Cortex and soredia C+ red (lecanoric acid). Locally abundant on exposed tree branches and rocks. Steeped in ammonia, this lichen is a good source of a deep purple dye.

129b Thallus lacking soredia. Fig. 378. ....
.... *Dendrographa leucophaea* (**Tuck.**) **Darb.**

Thallus whitish mineral gray, 6-20 cm long, stiff and brittle, pendulous on branches or rock; apothecia common. Cortex and medulla P+ deep red (protocetraric acid). Common in exposed areas. *D. minor* Darb. has the same chemistry but is much smaller (3-6 cm) with thin branches. There are several other nonsorediate fruticose lichens that occur only in this area. One, *Roccella fimbriata* Darb., is externally the

Figure 378.

same as *D. leucophaea* but reacts C+ red (lecanoric acid) and has a cortex of transverse rather than longitudinal hyphae, a microscopic character. Rare *Schizopelte californica* Th. Fr. has coarsely thickened branches and terminal apothecia with brown spores. *Teloschistes villosus* (Ach.) Norm, is densely covered with a fine tomentum visible under a hand lens.

130a Branches smooth, shiny, lacking phyllocladia or lobules. Fig. 379. ....*Sphaerophorus globosus* (**Huds.**) **Vain.**

Thallus light brown to tan, erect, 4-8 cm tall, rather stiff; apothecia spherical, at tips of branches, the disc sooty. Medulla iodine + blue (sphaerophorin also present). Common on humus and tree trunks in humid conifer forests and on soil in the Arctic. The overall aspect reminds one of *Cladonia* but the medulla is solid. *Sphaerophorus fragilis* (L.) Pers., an arctic species occurring as far south as New England, is sparsely branched and reacts iodine negative.

Figure 379.

130b Branches densely covered with tiny lobules (phyllocladia), dull (do not use hand lens). **131**

131a Pseudopodetia minute, 0.3-1.0 cm high, the phyllocladia granular or powdery; cephalodia lacking. Fig. 380. ....
....*Stereocaulon albicans* **Th. Fr.**

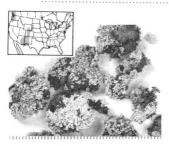

Figure 380.

Pseudopodetia white, fragile; phyllocladia granular, decorticate, cephalodia lacking. Medulla K+ yellow, P+ yellow (atranorin, psoromic acid, or thamnolic acid). Rare on soil and in rock crevices. A similar species, *S. microscopicum* (Vill.) Frey, has a yellowish cast (usnic acid). *S. subalbicans* Lamb has no central branches but consists of a granular mass of phyllocladia. Both are western species.

131b Pseudopodetia coarse, more than 1 cm high, the phyllocladia distinct, corticated; cephalodia often present. 132

132a Soredia present. Fig. 381. ....*Stereocaulon pileatum* **Ach.**

Figure 381.

Pseudopodetia whitish mineral gray, erect, simple or sparingly branched; primary thallus persistent; soredia apical, capitate; apothecia common. Medulla KC+ reddish, P+ pale yellow (atranorin and lobaric acid). Common on stones and fence rows in open fields. In New England there is a related species, *S. nanodes* Tuck., which has an erect sorediate primary thallus. In the Olympic Mountains of Washington one may find *S. spathuliferum* Vain., which has a poorly developed or evanescent primary thallus.

132b Soredia lacking. 133

133a Growing directly on rock, usually firmly attached. 134

133b Growing on soil or humus, more or less loosely attached. ..135

134a Phyllocladia all cylindric-coralloid (use hand lens). Fig. 382.
....*Stereocaulon dactylophyllum* Flk.

Pseudopodetia mineral gray, tufted, 2-6 cm tall; phyllocladia dense, tomentum thin or lacking; apothecia common, terminal. Medulla K+ yellow, P+ yellow orange (atranorin and stictic acid). Common on rocks in open outcrops. This species is frequently collected in the southern Appalachians. *S. intermedium* (Sav.) Magn., a rare species in the Pacific Northwest, is close except for chemistry (P−, lobaric acid).

Figure 382.

134b Phyllocladia flattened, squamulose or digitate-squamulose. Fig. 383. ....*Stereocaulon saxatile* Magn.
Pseudopodetia whitish mineral gray, loosely attached to adnate, 3-6 cm tall, often forming orbicular colonies; phyllocladia short, dense, the tomentum sparse to thick, gray; cephalodia sparse; apothecia common, terminal. Medulla KC+ reddish, P+ pale yellow (atranorin and lobaric acid). Common on boulders and stone fences in open areas. This species is frequently collected in the northern states. It inter-

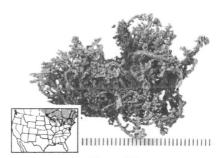

Figure 383.

grades broadly with *S. paschale,* which has numerous cephalodia. From New England to Nova Scotia it may occur with *S. glaucescens* Tuck., which has granulose to crenate-squamulose phyllocladia.

135a Primary thallus persistent as small squamules or granular crusts; pseudopodetia short, erect, 1-2 cm high. 136

135b Primary thallus evanescent or lacking; pseudopodetia taller, 2-6 cm long, prostrate or erect. 137

136a Cephalodia blackish brown, scabrid (use hand lens). Fig. 384. ....*Stereocaulon condensatum* **Hoffm.**

Pseudopodetia mineral gray, covering extensive areas of sandy soil, 1-2 cm high; phyllocladia dense, digitate, tomentum sparse; apothecia common, terminal. Medulla KC+ reddish, P+ pale yellow (atranorin and lobaric acid). Common on soil in fields and open areas. This is the only common *Stereocaulon* so closely attached to soil in eastern North America.

Figure 384.

136b Cephalodia reddish brown, smooth. Fig. 385. ....*Stereocaulon glareosum* **(Sav.) Magn.**

Pseudopodetia whitish mineral gray, 1-2 cm high, traces of primary thallus sometimes present; phyllocladia flattened, short, tomentum often well developed, whitish rosy; apothecia common, terminal. Medulla KC+ reddish, P+ pale yellow (atranorin and lobaric acid). Widespread on sandy soil in open areas. *S. incrustatum* Flk., a rare species in Colorado, differs in having thick gray tomentum in which the scattered phyllocladia are partially immersed.

Figure 385. (X3).

137a Tomentum on the branches conspicuous and continuous. Fig. 386. ....*Stereocaulon tomentosum* **Fr.**

Pseudopodetia whitish mineral gray, growing loosely on the substratum, prostrate to suberect, 4-8 cm tall; phyllocladia dense, digitate; cephalodia small, concealed in the tomentum; apothecia common, lateral. Medulla K+ yellow, P+ pale orange (atranorin and stictic acid). Common on soil over rocks and on humus. The thick tomentum and numerous lateral apothecia characterize this species. A chemical variant with lobaric acid (KC+ reddish) occurs in western North America with the typical form. Another western

Figure 386.

species with stictic acid, *S. myriocarpum* Th. Fr., differs in having large black cephalodia (1 mm across) and more appressed tomentum. It occurs from Washington and Montana southward into Mexico.

137b Tomentum sparse or lacking, surface of branches bare. 138

138a Cephalodia numerous, small, blackish, scabrid (use hand lens); pseudopodetia erect. Fig. 387. ....
....*Stereocaulon paschale* **(L.) Hoffm.**

Pseudopodetia whitish mineral gray, tufted or growing loosely on the substratum, 4-8 cm tall; phyllocladia dense, short and squamiform; apothecia common, mostly terminal. Medulla KC+ red, P+ pale yellow (atranorin and lobaric acid). Widespread on soil and among mosses. The range of this species overlaps that of *S. saxatile*, which has sparse inconspicuous cephalodia.

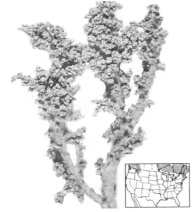

Figure 387. (X2).

138b Cephalodia rare, brownish, smooth; pseudopodetia decumbent. Fig. 388. ....*Stereocaulon rivulorum* **Magn.**

Pseudopodetia whitish mineral gray, forming low dense colonies, 2-4 cm broad; phyllocladia small, almost granular, cephalodia sparse; apothecia rare. Medulla KC+ red, P+ pale yellow (atranorin and lobaric acid). Rare on rock and soil in arctic regions.

Figure 388.

V. Squamulose Lichens

This is an artificial group of unrelated lichens that all have the squamulose growth form. Some are transitional to the crustose groups. The most frequently collected ones will be sterile *Cladonia* squamules, which when small (less than 0.5 cm long) cannot usually be identified to species with certainty. In such cases one must look for fertile specimens. The squamulose Lecideas and *Dermatocarpon lachneum* will be collected rather frequently on limey soil in open places, being quite common in desert regions.

1a Thallus yellowish to whitish or greenish mineral gray. 2

1b Thallus brown to dark brick red. 8

2a Squamules closely adnate on soil, contiguous. Fig. 389. ....
....*Squamarina lentigera* (Web.) **Poelt**

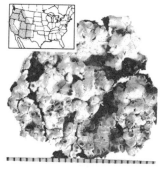

Squamules crowded, 1-3 mm wide, with a vague white rim, fragile, forming colonies 3-5 cm broad; apothecia common, the disc tan to light orangish brown. Cortex K+ yellow (atranorin). Widespread on calcareous soils, especially gypsum, in exposed areas. Do not confuse with the squamulose Lecideas (see below).

Figure 389.

2b Squamules suberect, loosely attached to free-growing. 3

3a Squamules with a greenish yellow cast above and below. ....
....*Cladonia robbinsii* (see p. 170)

3b Squamules not yellowish (at least below). 4

4a Squamules K+ deep yellow→red (test lower surface). ....
....*Cladonia subcariosa* (see p. 171)

4b Squamules K−, K+ very pale yellow, or brownish. 5

5a Growing loosely on white sand along the Gulf coast. Fig. 390.
....*Cladonia prostrata* **Evans**

Squamules very large, up to 3 cm long, curled upward at the margins when dry, the lower surface chalky white; podetia lacking but pycnidia common. K+ yellow (atranorin) and P+ red (fumarprotocetraric acid). Widespread on exposed beaches. This could be confused with no other *Cladonia*. Companion species are *C. evansii* and *C. leporina*.

Figure 390.

5b Growing more or less attached to soil or mosses. 6

6a Squamules very long and narrow (1-3 cm) with a blackened base; collected only in the Great Smoky Mountains. Fig. 391.
.............................*Gymnoderma lineare* (Evans) Yosh. & Sharp
Squamules dark greenish mineral gray; lower surface white to brownish toward the tips, weakly corticated; podetia lacking but small clustered apothecia common on lobe tips. K+ yellow (atranorin). This is one of the most unusual endemic lichens in North America and should not be collected by individuals. It was formerly called a *Cladonia*.

Figure 391.

6b Squamules shorter (to 1 cm), base not blackened; collected throughout eastern North America. 7

7a Squamules chalky white below. ....
.....*Cladonia apodocarpa* (see p. 171) or *C. turgida* (see p. 167)

7b Squamules grayish or in part darker below. ....
....*Cladonia mateocyatha*   (see p. 156)

8a Collected on tree bark. 9

8b Collected on soil, soil in rock crevices, or on burned trees or stumps. 10

9a Squamules 0.5 cm or more broad, black dots (perithecia) common. ....*Dermatocarpon tuckermanii* (see p. 102)

9b Squamules smaller, 0.5-1.0 mm wide; apothecia present. Fig. 392. ....*Pannaria leucosticta* (Tuck.) Nyl.
Thallus·composed of numerous confluent squamules, 3-6 cm broad; margins white pruinose with raised finger-like projections; lower surface rather dark, tomentose; apothecia common, the rim white. On deciduous trees, rarely on rocks, in mature forests. It is inconspicuous and not commonly collected. There is some intergradation with *Pannaria rubiginosa*, which is larger and lacks white pruina.

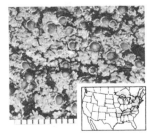

Figure 392.

10a Squamules sorediate (use hand lens); common on charred stumps. Fig. 393. ....*Lecidea scalaris* (Ach.) Ach.

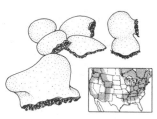

Figure 393. (X8).

Squamules about 1 mm long, forming crowded colonies several cm wide, somewhat ascending and hoop-shaped (under lens), sorediate on the lower surface; apothecia rare. Medulla C+, KC+ red (lecanoric acid). Common on dead wood and charred stumps. Another similar species but without soredia is *Lecidea friesii* Ach., which is C—; it grows on charred wood.

10b Squamules not sorediate; common on soil. 11

11a Upper surface with numerous black dots (perithecia); apothecia never present. Fig. 394. ....
........................*Dermatocarpon lachneum* (Ach.) A. L. Sm.

Figure 394.

Squamules dark brown, 1-3 mm wide or more, rather closely adnate on soil, crowded, forming colonies 3-8 cm broad; perithecia common. Common on soil among boulders or in rock crevices. Calcareous soils are definitely preferred by this extremely variable lichen. In desert regions it consolidates the soil. Several species in this group have been reported from North America but all probably belong to *D. lachneum.*

11b Upper surface with few if any black dots but apothecia often present. 12

12a Squamules roundish, often with a whitish rim. Fig. 395. ....
....*Lecidea rubiformis* (Ach.) Wahlenb.

Figure 395. (X5).

Squamules brown but sometimes turning white pruinose, 2-4 mm wide, forming loose colonies 1-4 cm broad; apothecia sometimes present, brown or black without a rim. Common on limestone outcrops and calcareous soil. This species is representative of a whole group of squamulose Lecideas that are sometimes referred to as *Psora.* One species, *L. icterica* (Mont.) Tayl., for example, has a brilliant yellow medulla. Weber (1963) has constructed keys to species in this general group.

12b Squamules lobate, without any white rim. Fig. 396. ....
.... *Heppia lutosa* (Ach.) Nyl.

Squamules brown to greenish olive, 2-6 mm wide, scattered to more or less organized into a lobate colony; algae blue-green; apothecia common. Widespread on calcareous soil but often overlooked. This strange genus is highly developed in semidesert regions of western North America where several other species are found. *Heppia euploca* (Ach.) Vain. will be rarely collected on rock; it has an umbilicate attachment and a sorediate margin.

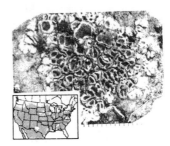

Figure 396.

LIST OF SYNONYMS AND INCORRECT NAMES

The names of many common lichens have changed because taxonomic research has shown them to be incorrect. In these cases a more appropriate but often little-known name must be substituted for a familiar but illegitimate name. This is an unfortunate but necessary step in botanical progress. Other name changes are the result of more accurate determinations. The following list gives the more important names used in Fink's *Lichen Flora of the United States*, Nearing's *Lichen Book*, and Hale's *Lichen Handbook* and their correct equivalents in this book. Most herbaria will use the older names. A recent checklist by Hale and Culberson (Bryologist 69: 141-182. 1966) that can be obtained from Duke University contains a complete list of synonyms.

Old Name	Correct Name
Alectoria chalybeiformis	= A. nidulifera
Alectoria jubata	= A. americana + A. nadvornikiana
Anaptychia aquila	= A. palmatula
Anaptychia comosa	= A. echinata
Anaptychia galactophylla	= A. echinata
Anaptychia heterochroa	= A. obscurata
Cetraria collata	= Cetrelia chicitae
Cetraria crispa	= C. ericetorum
Cetraria glauca	= Platismatia glauca
Cetraria herrei	= Platismatia herrei
Cetraria juniperina	= C. canadensis + C. viridis
Cetraria lacunosa	= Platismatia lacunosa + P. tuckermanii
Cetraria stenophylla	= Platismatia stenophylla
Cetraria tuckermanii	= Platismatia tuckermanii
Cladonia alpicola	= C. macrophylla
Cladonia cornutoradiata	= C. subulata
Cladonia linearis	= Gymnoderma lineare
Cladonia mitrula	= C. capitata
Cladonia sylvatica	= C. arbuscula
Dermatocarpon aquaticum	= D. fluviatile
Dermatocarpon arboreum	= D. tuckermanii
Dermatocarpon hepaticum	= D. lachneum
Evernia vulpina	= Letharia vulpina
Gyrophora dillenii	= Umbilicaria mammulata
Lecanora lentigera	= Squamarina lentigera
Lecanora rubina	= L. chrysoleuca
Lecidea russellii	= L. rubiformis
Leptogium tremelloides	= L. cyanescens
Lobaria verrucosa	= L. scrobiculata
Nephroma "laevigatum"	= N. bellum
Nephroma lusitanicum	= N. laevigatum
Parmelia aspera	= Parmelia exasperata

Parmelia cetrarioides = Cetrelia cetrarioides + C. olivetorum
Parmelia cladonia = Pseudevernia cladonia
Parmelia colpodes = Anzia colpodes
Parmelia conspurcata = P. subargentifera
Parmelia coralloidea = P. tinctorum
Parmelia enteromorpha = Hypogymnia enteromorpha
Parmelia finkii = P. obsessa
Parmelia furfuracea = Pseudevernia consocians
Parmelia leucochlora = P. congruens
Parmelia pertusa = Menegazzia terebrata
Parmelia physodes = Hypogymnia physodes
Parmelia saximontana = P. substygia
Parmelia sphaerospora = P. congruens
Parmelia stenophylla = P. taractica
Parmelia sublaevigata = P. galbina + P. livida
Peltigera scutata = P. collina
Physcia aegialita = Dirinaria aegialita
Physcia aspera = Dirinaria aspera
Physcia frostii = Dirinaria frostii
Physcia obscura = P. ciliata
Physcia picta = Dirinaria picta
Physcia purpurascens = Dirinaria purpurascens
Physcia tribacia = P. millegrana
Ramalina dilacerata = R. minuscula
Ramalina pollinariella = R. roesleri
Ramalina yemensis = R. ecklonii
Stereocaulon coralloides = S. dactylophyllum
Stereocaulon evolutoides = S. saxatile
Sticta amplissima = Lobaria quercizans
Sticta aurata = Pseudocyphellaria aurata
Sticta crocata = Pseudocyphellaria crocata
Umbilicaria pustulata = U. papulosa
Usnea sorediifera = U. fulvoreagens

Acknowledgments for Illustrations

Abbayes, H. des: 402, 405, 407-9 (Traité de Lichenologie, Le-Chavalier, 1951).

Asahina, Y.: 2, 249, 272 (Illustrated Flora of Japanese Cryptogams, 1939).

Frey, E.: 58, 381, 384, 385, 388 (Kabenhorst Kryptogamenflora, vol. 9, 1933, 1934).

Grassi, M.: 7, 9, 15, 399 (Lilloa, vol. 25, 1950).

Hale, M. E.: 1 (Lichen Handbook, 1961); 18 (Biology of Lichens, 1967).

Halliday, N.: 28, 32, 39, 40, 79, 137, 150, 178, 196, 242, 253, 263, 265, 266, 269, 270, 274, 278, 281, 284, 286, 288, 290, 291, 293, 295-7, 300-3, 307, 308, 310-12, 321, 323-7, 338, 339, 341, 390, 391, 403, 404, 410, 416, 418, 420, 424, 426, 427 (originals).

Harris, C. W.: 27, 346, 359 (Bryologist, vol. 4, 1900).

Henssen, A.: 371 (Symb. Bot. Ups. 18, 1963).

Howard, G.: 152, 156, 264, 271, 331 (Bryologist, vol. 66, 1963).

Lindahl, P. O.: 37, 428 (Svensk Bot. Tidskr. vol. 47, 1953).

Menez, E.: 4, 50, 53, 54, 67, 74, 76, 81, 92, 108, 132, 138, 139, 155, 181, 191, 202, 204, 211, 333, 393, 395, 398, 401, 411, 412 (originals).

Motyka, J.: 56, 65, 110, 165, 172, 174, 175, 353, 354, 370, 372 (Flora Polska, vol. 5, 1960, 1962).

Riddle, L. W.: 417 (Bot. Gaz. vol. 50, 1910).

Schneider, A.: 222, 237, 330, 379, 414, 419, 422, 423 (A Textbook of Lichenology, 1897).

Schroeder, J.: 17, 26, 35, 38, 44, 52, 67, 75, 95, 96, 102, 105, 106, 111, 112, 115, 117, 130, 133, 135, 144, 149, 153, 158, 164, 168, 170, 171, 179, 186, 188, 192, 195, 197, 206, 223, 227, 230, 234, 241, 248, 250, 256, 257, 299, 329, 332, 336, 344, 365, 376 (originals).

Schumacher, E.: 120, 147, 237, 330 (originals).

Tateoka, S.: 25, 57, 80, 84, 190, 342, 343 (originals).

Trass, H.: 259, 261, 262, 268, 273, 275-7, 279, 280, 282, 283, 285, 289, 304-6, 314-16 (Lood. Selts Eesti Tead. Juures, vol. 5, 1958).

INDEX AND PICTURED-GLOSSARY

A

Abortive: imperfect or poorly developed, as podetia in some Cladonias.

Acarospora
hilaris, 9

ACICULAR: long and needle-shaped, as spores. Fig. 397.

Figure 397.

Adnate: lying flat on and attached to the substratum.

Agrestia
hispida, 182

Alectoria
americana, 194
bicolor, 196
chalybeiformis, 208
crinalis, 191
fremontii, 193
implexa, 192
jubata, 208
nadvornikiana, 193
nidulifera, 193
ochroleuca, 192
oregana, 194
positiva, 193
sarmentosa, 192
simplicior, 193

ALGAL LAYER: a thin layer of green or blue-green algae lying just below the upper cortex. See Fig. 7.

Anaptychia
appalachensis, 50
aquila, 208
casarettiana, 51
comosa, 208
echinata, 104
erinacea, 104
galactophylla, 208
granulifera, 77
heterochroa, 208
hypoleuca, 104
kaspica, 103
leucomelaena, 50
obscurata, 51

palmatula, 105
ravenelii, 49
speciosa, 51
squamulosa, 105

ANNULATE: ringed, referring to cracks in the cortex of Usneas. Fig. 398.

Figure 398.

Anzia
colpodes, 111
ornata, 57

Apical: at the terminal part of a lobe or podetium.

Apothecia: the reproductive structures of ascomycetes containing the hymenium (asci, spores, and paraphyses), usually disc- or cup-shaped.

Appressed: lying flat on and firmly attached to the substratum.

Aquatic: growing in or near water.

Areolate: composed of areoles, as the podetial surface of some Cladonias or the thallus of some crustose lichens.

Areoles: small discrete corticated greenish patches on the thallus surface.

Articulated: jointed or segmented, as the branches of some Usneas.

ASCUS: a sac (20-100μ long) containing spores. Fig. 399.

Figure 399.

Axil: the upper angle between branches of fruticose lichens.

213

B

Biseriate: arranged in two rows, as spores in an ascus.
BULBATE: inflated, as the basally inflated cilia in some *Parmelia* species. Fig. 400.

Figure 400.

C

Calcareous: containing calcium or lime.
CAPITATE: shaped like a head, referring to soralia. Fig. 401.

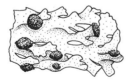

Figure 401.

CEPHALODIA: tiny thalli (0.5-1.0 mm) growing on the upper cortex in *Peltigera*, *Placopsis*, and *Stereocaulon*. Fig. 402.

Figure 402.

CHANNELED: grooved, as the lower surface of *Pseudevernia*. Fig. 403.

Figure 403.

Chinky: cracked and fissured.
CILIA: hair-like outgrowths along
the margins of lobes. Fig. 404.

Figure 404.

Ciliate: provided with cilia.

Coalesce: fuse together, as many thalli merging into a single large colony.

Coccocarpia
cronia, 81
parmelioides, 111

Coenogonium
implexum, 184
interplexum, 184
interpositum, 184
linkii, 184
moniliforme, 184

Collema
bachmanianum, 132
callibotrys, 131
coccophorum, 132
conglomeratum, 131
crispum, 128, 132
cristatum, 128
cyrtaspis, 131
flaccidum, 128
fragrans, 131
furfuraceum, 128
leptaleum, 131
leucopeplum, 130
limosum, 132
microptychium, 131
multipartitum, 131
nigrescens, 130
polycarpon, 131
ryssoleum, 132
subfurfuraceum, 128
subfurvum, 128
subnigrescens, 130
tenax, 132
tunaeforme, 128

Colony: a group of lichen thalli growing together.

Contiguous: touching or in close contact, as lobes.

Continuous: unbroken, as a cortex without pores or cracks.

CORALLOID: resembling coral, as richly branched isidia. Fig. 405.

Figure 405.

Cord: a dense strand of hyphae making up the center of branches in *Usnea*.

Coriaceous: leathery and not easily broken or crumbled.

Cornicularia
aculeata, 196
californica, 194
divergens, 196
normoerica, 195

CORTEX: the outermost layer of the thallus consisting of compressed hyphal cells that appear to be cellular. See Fig. 7.

Corticate: having a cortex.

Corticolous: growing on tree trunks or branches.

Crenate: having a notched edge, as lobe margins.

Crustose: a lichen growth form, thalli growing in intimate contact with the substratum and lacking a lower cortex and rhizines.

Cyphellae: large circular pores in the lower surface of *Sticta*.

D

Dactylina
arctica, 148
madreporiformis, 148
ramulosa, 149

Decorticate: lacking any cortex, leaving the medulla directly exposed.

Dendrographa
leucophaea, 199
minor, 199

Dentate: a toothed edge, as lobe margins.

Dermatocarpon
aquaticum, 208
arboreum, 208
fluviatile, 99
hepaticum, 208
lachneum, 206
miniatum, 139
moulinsii, 137
reticulatum, 137
tuckermanii, 102

DICHOTOMOUS: dividing into two parts, as a forking branching pattern in the rhizines of foliose lichens. See Fig. 94.

Diffuse: scattered and without any definite pattern, as diffuse soredia.

Digitate: arranged like fingers.

Dirinaria
aegialita, 114
aspera, 61
frostii, 62
picta, 61
purpurascens, 115

Disc: the surface of apothecia.

Discrete: separate and distinct, as lobes or thalli.
Dissected: cut up or divided into many lobes or lobules.
Dorsiventral: having distinct upper and lower surfaces that are different.

E

Eciliate: lacking cilia.
Ecorticate: lacking a cortex, as the lower surface of *Cladonia* squamules and some Anaptychias.
Ellipsoidal: shaped like an ellipse, usually referring to spores.
Endemic: occurring only in a single small geographic area.
Entire: smooth and unbroken, without notches, referring to lobe margins.

Esorediate: lacking soredia.
Evanescent: disappearing at maturity, as the primary thallus of some Cladonias.

Expanded: spread out, as the thallus of large foliose lichens.

F

Farinose: powdery as flour, referring to soredia.
Fibrillose: having fibrils.
FIBRILS: short simple lateral branches, as in *Usnea*. Fig. 406.

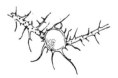

Figure 406.

Fibrous: composed of fibers, hyphae which run parallel as in the cortex of *Anaptychia*, best seen under a microscope.
FILAMENTOUS: a lichen growth form, thin hair-like strands of filamentous algae and fungi as in *Coenogonium* and *Ephebe*. See Fig. 349.
Fissured: deeply cracked, as in the cortex of some foliose and fruticose lichens.
Foliose: a lichen growth form, referring to leaf-like thalli.
Fruticose: a lichen growth form, shrubby or hair-like.
Fungus: a colorless plant consisting of thread-like hyphae.
FURCATE: regularly forked, referring to branching patterns of lobes and podetia. See Fig. 6A.
Fusiform: spindle-shaped, usually referring to spores.

G

Gelatinous: like jelly or gelatin, used to describe unstratified lichens with blue-green algae when wet.
Granular: grain-like, used to describe coarse soredia or certain subcrustose thalli.

H

HAIR: fine multicellular outgrowths from the cortex, as in *Physcia ciliata*. See Fig. 204.

HYPHAE: microscopic multicellular threads that make up the fungus or lichen plant body. Fig. 407.

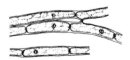

Figure 407.

I

Imperforate: lacking holes, used in describing closed axils of branches or discs of apothecia.
Incised: deeply notched, as the margins of lobes or squamules.
Irregular: uneven, referring to lobe margins of foliose lichens.
ISIDIA: finger-like cylindrical outgrowths from the upper cortex. Fig. 408.

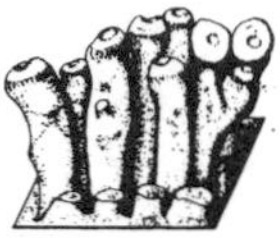

Figure 408.

L

LABRIFORM: lip-shaped, usually referring to apical soralia of foliose lichens. Fig. 409.

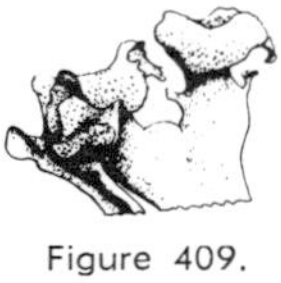

Figure 409.

Lacerate: having jagged edges or tips, as lobe margins and podetia.
Laciniate: divided into numerous small segments or lobes.
Lamellae: thin plates, referring to acid crystals.
Laminal: superficial on the surface of thallus or lobes, as soralia or apothecia.

LINEAR: narrow and uniform in width, as lobes or soralia. Fig. 410.

Figure 410.

Lobate: consisting of many lobes, referring usually to the thallus margin of certain crustose lichens.
LOBE: a rounded or linear division of the thallus. Fig. 411.

Figure 413.

Mottled: variegated white and black or brown, as on the lower surface of some foliose lichens.
MURIFORM: spores divided into many chambers by transverse and longitudinal walls. Fig. 414.

Figure 411.

Lobule: a subdivision of a lobe.

Figure 414.

M

MARGINAL: located at or along the margins of lobes, as soralia. Fig. 412.

Figure 412.

Markings: whitish reticulate or spotted outlines on the surface of lobes.
MEDULLA: the inner part of the thallus, between the algal layer and the lower cortex or lower surface, consisting of loosely interwoven hyphae. See Fig. 7.
Membrane: a thin covering over the cup-shaped podetia of Cladonia.
MICROCONIDIA: uninucleate baciliform cells produced in pycnidia. Fig. 413.

N

Nodulose: having nodules, small knots in the branches.
NOSTOC: a blue-green alga which forms filaments of chains of cells. Fig. 415.

Figure 415.

O

P

PAPILLAE: small bumps on the upper cortex, as in *Ramalina* and *Usnea* species, or on the lower surface of foliose lichens. Fig. 416.

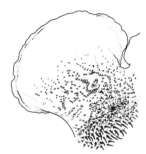

Figure 416.

Papillate: having papillae.
PARAPHYSES: thread-like hyphae packing the spaces between asci in the hymenium. See Fig. 399.

Pendulous: hanging down.
Perforate: pierced with holes.
Perithecia: flask-shaped fruiting bodies of pyrenocarpous lichens.
Perlatolic acid, 17
PHYLLOCLADIA: tiny granular or lobed leaf-like structures on the branches of *Stereocaulon*. Fig. 417.

Figure 417. (X4).

Plane: flat and smooth, referring to
  the surface of lobes.
Plates: flattened rhizine-like structures on the lower surface of
  some Umbilicarias.
PODETIUM: a hollow simple or
  branched upright structure in
  Cladonia. Fig. 418.

PSEUDOCYPHELLAE: simple pores
  in the upper or lower cortex.
  See Fig. 5C.
PSEUDOPODETIUM: the upright
  fruticose thallus of *Stereocaulon*
  and *Baeomyces*, Fig. 419.

Figure 419.

Psoromic acid, 17
Pulvic anhydride, 17
Pulvinate: growing in small cushions.
Punctiform: shaped like a dot, as
  tiny orbicular soralia.
PUSTULAR: blister-like. Fig. 420.

Figure 420.

PUSTULATE: covered with small
  blisters. See Fig. 48D.
PYCNIDIA: flask-shaped reproductive structures within the medulla that produce microconidia.
  See Fig. 14C.

R

Figure 418.

Primary thallus: the squamulose or
  granular thallus of *Cladonia*.
Proliferate: to produce parts in suc-
  cession, as the cups in certain
  Cladonias.
Prostrate: lying flat on the substra-
  tum.
Protocetraric acid, 17
Protolichesterinic acid, 17
PRUINA: a fine white woolly cover-
  ing on the upper cortex. See
  Fig. 5D.

RETICULATE: in a network arrangement, as cracks in the upper cortex. See Fig. 5A.
REVOLUTE: rolled downward, as tips of sorediate lobes. See Fig. 107.
RHIZINES: strands of hyphae on the lower surface of many foliose lichens. Fig. 421.

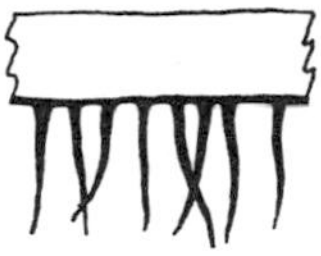

Figure 421.

Rhodophyscin, 17
Rimose: finely chinked or fissured.
ROTUND: rounded in outline, as the tips of broad lobes. See Fig. 67.
Rugose: having wrinkles or ridges.

S

Saxicolous: growing on rocks.
Scabrid: having fine scales on the upper cortex.
SEPARATE: not joined or in close contact, referring to patterns of lobing of the thallus. See Fig. 4.
SEPTATE: divided into two or more parts by a septum or wall, as septate spores. Fig. 422.

Figure 422.

Sessile: attached directly on the thallus without a stalk.
Soralia: clumps of soredia on the surface or margins of the thallus.
Soredia: microscopic clumps of several algal cells surrounded by hyphae and erupting at the surface of the thallus.
Spinulate: provided with spinules.
Spinules: short stiff pointed branchlets.
SPORES: microscopic reproductive cells of fungi contained in the asci. Fig. 423.

Figure 423.

Figure 425.

Stipe: a stalk that supports the fruiting body of certain fungi.

STRATIFIED: consisting of horizontal layers, referring to the internal structure of lichens which have a distinct cortex, algal layer, and medulla, and frequently a lower cortex and rhizines. Fig. 426.

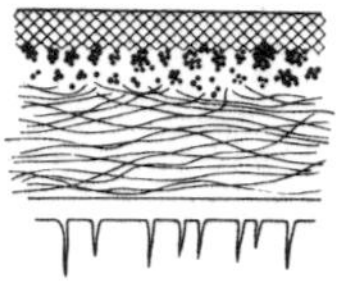

Figure 424.

Squamule: a small scale-like thallus which lacks a lower cortex and rhizines.

Squamulose: a lichen growth form, referring to thalli consisting of squamules.

Squarrose: a kind of branching pattern of rhizines. See Fig. 93A.

Figure 426.

Strepsilin, 17

Striae: elongate white ridges (0.1-1.0 mm long) in the cortex of *Alectoria* and *Ramalina.*

Striate: provided with striae.

Subcrustose: a growth form intermediate between crustose and foliose, usually with a typically crustose central part and a lobed thallus margin.

Suberect: ascending toward the edges of the thallus but prostrate at the center; a growth form intermediate between foliose and fruticose.

Subfruticose: a growth form intermediate between foliose and fruticose.

Subisidiate: sparsely or imperfectly isidiate, often with intermingled soredia.

Subsquamulose: sparsely or imperfectly squamulose.

Substratum: the medium (soil, rock, humus, bark, or dead wood) on which a lichen grows.

T

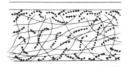

Figure 427.

Figure 428.

W

WHITE-RETICULATE: having a netted pattern of white lines, as the surface of lobe tips in certain foliose lichens. See Fig. 5B.

WHITE-SPOTTED: having numerous tiny white spots on the upper cortex. See Fig. 5C.

X

Xanthoria
    candelaria, 40
    fallax, 40
    parietina, 88
    polycarpa, 88
Zeorin, 17